CHRISTMAS IN FRANCE

A French child places her slippers at the fireplace on Christmas Eve. Père Noël will soon come to fill them up with toys and goodies.

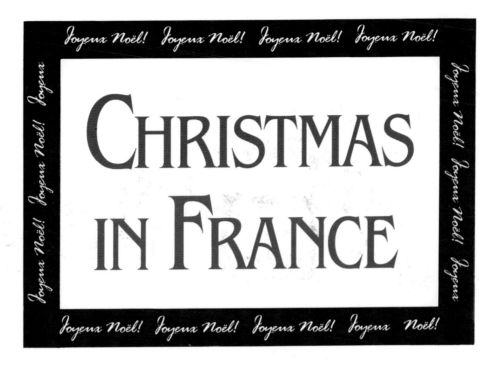

CHRISTMAS IN FRANCE

Corinne Madden Ross

PASSPORT BOOKS
a division of *NTC Publishing Group*
Lincolnwood, Illinois USA

Text consultant
Réal de Mélogue
Directeur-Général de l'Alliance française–Maison française
de Chicago

Food and crafts consultant
Marcelle M. Devane
Chairman, Groupe folklorique de l'Alliance française–Maison
française de Chicago

The editors wish to thank all the members of the Alliance
française–Maison française de Chicago who helped with the
development of this publication. Special thanks to Florence
Petacque Stern, who contributed the recipes appearing on
page 70, and to Janis Notz, whose cooperation was invaluable
during the photographing of the recipe cards. We also wish
to acknowledge the French Cultural Services for research
assistance throughout the project.

1992 Printing

Contents

INTRODUCTION

Noël. Few French words possess such richly evocative power. If I used Noël in a game of idea associations, it would conjure up at once, in one tumbling mass, a crowd of varied, often stereotyped images—religious as well as nonreligious. Thus, if someone said "crèche," I would think, all at the same instant: the Infant Jesus, the Three Kings, and the midnight Mass. And I could not help recalling Daudet's story of Father Balaguère, who hastened through the three Christmas Masses while dreaming of tempting, sumptuous fare.

At the mention of "toys," the image of the generous Père Noël would certainly come to my mind, along with that of the fabulous shop windows in front of which kids, after school, come gaping with wonder and yearning. Surely if someone said "Christmas feast," I would see, through the eyes of my memory, the incredible choice of birds of all feathers suspended at the store where the merchant also sells truffles and foie gras. Next door to the shop of the candy maker, whose fine chocolates each year provoke waves of indigestion in the entire community— the famous *mal au foie* that only French people seem to know about! In short, I would reexperience all the very obvious charm, somehow familiar to all, of Noël—its public face.

But there is also, I believe, in each of us a unique, intimate understanding of the holiday carried by some childhood memory—still alive, precise, untouched. Thus, for me, Noël is forever linked, in the memory of my heart, to the little town in the Jura Mountains where I grew up: a town blessed among all since each year snow fell, sometimes abundantly, before Christmas. The snow seemed to us—to us children—like a supreme favor from heaven! So the fir trees, with their pretty garlands, which the shopkeepers had decoratively lined up along the main street at the beginning of December, would then assume their most natural and at the same time festive look. It was like walking down the Royal Way when going to midnight Mass. The snow squeaked under our footsteps and our breaths formed light clouds in the cold air, just as in the books. By comparison the church, however poorly heated, always seemed to us deliciously warm thanks to the presence of the exceptional number of parishioners who—be it through devotion or tradition—filled our church of Saint-Bénigne each December 24. A no-less-unusual riot of lights made our eyes crinkle. And then the service would begin.

An increasing, almost palpable impatience would build up as the time approached that the entire congregation had been waiting for: when the booming voice of Mr. Duruy would explode into "Oh, Holy Night," finally breaking the silence filled only with our expectation and our nervous coughs, while easily dominating the organ that pompously accompanied him. It always was a very solemn moment, even if more than one among the faithful, year after year, waited for the "squeak" that would put to pieces the prestige our local baritone derived from this annual lyrical exhibition!

After returning home, my mother, to warm us up, would offer us a rare delight: a glass of hot wine scented with cinnamon. Then, in all conformity with tradition, my younger sister and I would place our shoes—our "Sunday best," of course—under the fir tree that had decorated a corner of the room since the day before, and whose candles we would not light until the next day.

I do not know to this day whether it was through fatigue or as a matter of principle, but in my family we never had réveillon after midnight Mass: instead, we celebrated the gastronomic ritual of the holiday on Christmas Day itself.

Dare I admit that I feel a great nostalgia for the strict observance of those rituals? Yes, indeed, I miss them, those exquisite love-feasts that, in the true spirit of Christmas, reunited all the family, cousins and uncles included—without ever forgetting the lonesome or the hard-to-please. Certainly, one says that all begins and all ends at the table in France; but beyond even the pleasures of the palate, the feeling of well-being that arose from those reunions seems to me, even now, the best testimony of the happy atmosphere that Noël brings about in France. And, in my opinion, it is neither a lesser mystery nor a small miracle that children and adults, believers and non-believers alike, share, at Christmastime, the same joy and thrills in a common experience that transcends them all.

Michèle Fieschi

Angels announce the Nativity to French shepherds in this fifteenth-century illuminated French manuscript.

Mme Fieschi is the wife of the former Consul-General of Chicago. While she resided in Chicago, she was an active participant in all French cultural activities in the area.

NOEL COMES TO FRANCE

Noël! That is the lovely French word for Christmas. It means "the birthday of Christ," and the people of France celebrate it with deep religious devotion. Noël is observed throughout the land with beautiful midnight Masses, charming manger scenes, and countless reenactments of the Nativity.

Signs that Noël is approaching begin to appear in France right after December 6, the feast day of Saint Nicholas, and continue through January 6, the Epiphany. The entire winter holiday season is a joyous one of merrymaking, gatherings with family and friends, Christmas decorations, and delicious holiday foods.

But Noël itself is a time for children to enjoy. The French cherish childhood as a time of innocence to safeguard for as long as possible. A child, filled with Christmas wonder and joy, is a sacred reminder of the innocence of the Christ Child whose birthday is commemorated. For grown-ups, preparing for Christmas is like recapturing one's own long-past childhood.

The French know Christmas is near when they begin to see *sapins,* or Christmas trees, at the outdoor flower markets, standing in pleasant-smelling rows like miniature forests. Having Christmas trees is not so widespread a custom in France as in some countries, but they have become more and more popular in recent years.

The trees come in all sizes: some are tall and bushy, others are table-top size—the better to fit into a small apartment. Whichever type, the trees very often will be potted. The French are a practical people. Potted trees not only last longer, but they may be replanted out-of-doors after the holidays are over.

It is often somewhat of a challenge to select just the right tree, but carrying it home can be a real prob-

After December 6, the figure of Père Noël begins to appear on the windows of shops and restaurants to wish Parisians happy holidays (above). An unusual coating of snow turns the grounds around the Eiffel Tower into a festive holiday playground for vacationing schoolchildren (right).

*This Parisian flower vendor offers a
magnificent grouping of mistletoe at
the Quai aux Fleurs, near Notre
Dame Cathedral.*

lem. Trying to stuff a stubborn fresh tree into an
automobile—or, worse still, into a taxi—can stretch
one's patience. But the French can be seen doing both
as Noël draws near.

In addition to Christmas trees, French outdoor
flower markets and flower shops offer a wealth of
other lovely decorations for the household. There are
branches of fir, some plain and others flocked, and
prickly boughs of holly. Mistletoe is almost a Christmas necessity, appearing in great bunches. The custom goes back to the ancient Celts, some of whom
lived in the area of France.

The Celts believed that mistletoe, with its shiny,
waxy berries and dusky evergreen leaves, symbolized
immortality. It was also thought to have miraculous
powers of healing. The Celtic priests treated the
plant with great reverence.

The mistletoe they sought often grew high at the
top of great oak trees. The priests cut the boughs
down with a golden sickle and never allowed them to
touch the earth. As the boughs dropped, they were
caught below in a pure white cloth.

Today the French consider mistletoe a good luck
charm. Young men and women have an even better
reason for liking it. Hung in branches around the
house, the festive plant provides an excellent oppor-

At this flower market alongside La Madeleine church in Paris, a Christmas hostess decides to purchase a few dried flowers to place among the fresh in her réveillon centerpiece.

tunity for claiming a holiday kiss. In some areas, mistletoe is gathered on Christmas Eve and then brought back to decorate the house or, in the country, even the stable.

Of all Christmas decorations, however, the most important are flowers. No French housewife considers her holiday table complete without a lavish arrangement of some kind. Guests bring flowers, too, as a gesture of thanks to their hostess. Roses, gladioli, carnations, and snapdragons are favorite Christmas choices, along with a wide variety of dried flowers. Potted plants are also popular: red and white poinsettias, sweet-smelling hyacinths, multicolored azaleas, and Christmas begonias.

In some parts of France a very special flower graces the Christmas table. It is called the hellebore—a tiny blossom with creamy white petals, glossy leaves, and a dark green stem. The French call it the Christmas rose.

There's a lovely old legend about how this flower came to be, and how it got its special name. The story tells about a young bellringer named Nicaise, who lived in a village near Rouen. Nicaise was dull witted.

His guardian, a poor parish priest named Father Anthime, frequently scolded him for his foolishness. Once on Christmas Eve, after an especially severe scolding, Nicaise sadly went up into the church tower until it was time to ring the bells for the midnight Mass. He soon fell fast asleep.

The church tower was ornamented with several ugly gargoyles, stone rainspouts carved to look like horrible beasts with their tongues sticking out. As Nicaise slept, he dreamed one of the gargoyles came to life.

The gargoyle spoke to him, saying that it was actually the Devil. The gargoyle told Nicaise that it liked him, which pleased the boy. Nicaise was not terribly bright, please remember.

Then the gargoyle offered Nicaise three wishes. Nicaise thought a bit. Finally, he said: "I'd like to be smart, that's one. And rich, that's two. And married to a beautiful lady. That's three."

A mother and child marvel over the hundreds of crèche figures for sale at the Christmas market in Strasbourg (above). Near them, another buyer selects new ornaments with care and a touch of frustration at the number of glittering bulbs from which she must choose (right).

The gargoyle agreed. Then Nicaise remembered that it was Christmas, and there were no flowers to decorate Father Anthime's little church.

"Please," he begged. "I also want some flowers for Father Anthime to place at the altar tonight."

The gargoyle spat with rage. That was too much. It told Nicaise to make do with what he already had been given. And the gargoyle added that it expected a little something in return. It demanded Nicaise's soul, in fact.

The gargoyle told the boy that it would return in exactly one year's time to take him away. "Unless," it laughed nastily, "unless on Christmas Eve one year from now, you can make flowers bloom in the snow!"

Nicaise woke up. What a strange dream, he thought. But was it really a dream? For as the months went by, all three wishes came true.

The full year passed, and it was once again Christmas Eve. Nicaise knew the Devil was coming for him that night. Frightened, he confessed his sins to Father Anthime.

The priest was horrified. "You've sold your soul," he cried, "and the Devil's coming to get you this very night—unless, by some miracle, you can actually make flowers bloom in the snow outside. My son, pray. Pray to the Good Lord, the angels, the saints, and to our Lord Jesus!"

The two knelt and prayed together as the midnight hour approached. Finally, thinking that the end was near, Nicaise crept sadly up the stairs to ring the bells one last time.

Just as he started to reach for the bell rope, he heard a cry from down below. Some children had wandered into the small church garden and they had found, of all things, flowers in the snow! Father Anthime came running, and when he saw the flowers, he began to weep.

"Nicaise," he called. "Come down, you are saved! We have won against the Devil. The Christ Child has sent flowers, real flowers—Christmas roses—to bloom in the snow!"

Many French families already have collections of tree ornaments, but it is great fun to go shopping for some new additions. Special stalls in the outdoor markets sell them, as do department stores. There are rows upon rows of shimmering baubles: shiny globes, frosted and plain, graceful bells in glowing colors, exotic birds, tiny angels, and replicas of Père Noël, the French Father Christmas.

Children love the small knitted or crocheted figures of animals, elves, and stars. There is tinsel, too,

On the pine-covered hills of Provence, children gather moss, stones, and branches for use in their family crèche.

in gold and silver. Even paper fish are sometimes sold as Christmas ornaments. They represent the golden carp, once a symbol of long life. Nowadays, the fish is a symbol of the New Year.

The tree is usually decorated a few days before Christmas, and it is seldom overloaded with ornaments. The entire family eagerly participates, especially the children.

The littlest children stand tall to help place ornaments, and perhaps gilded pine cones and walnuts, on whichever branches the children can reach. Sometimes, with their mother's help, they make little paper flowers, stars, or swans. These are hung with great care. At the top, Papa places a star, an image of Père Noël, or perhaps a treasured and somewhat tattered angel. Tinsel garlands add a pretty finishing touch.

Most French families adorn their trees with colored or white electric lights, but some still prefer real candles, usually red. They are lighted only for a short time and carefully watched to avoid fire. Often the hearth is decorated, too, with ornaments, paper garlands or bunches of red ribbon, and candles. And there may be mistletoe somewhere in the room, brightened by a red bow.

Popular as the Christmas tree has become, it takes second place to the most important symbol of French Christmas: the *crèche,* or manger scene. Churches set up their crèches sometime in the weeks preceding Christmas. Many crèches are magnificent, ornate displays; others are merely simple groupings of the Holy Family.

To children, the crèche is both a small world of fantasy and the focus of their devotion to the story of Christ's birth. The home crèche is set up a few days before Christmas, along with the tree. It is placed in a corner of the living room, on a table, or sometimes near the hearth.

Some families are fortunate enough to own antique crèche figures. These are often passed down from generation to generation, lovingly preserved and carefully unwrapped when it is time to set up the scene. Other families have simple manger scenes, with only a few figures. Imagination and personal taste are two important factors in how the crèche is presented.

Miniature figures for the crèche are also sold in department stores and in booths at the markets. On display are little images of Joseph and Mary, angels, shepherds, and the Three Wise Men, called the "Three Kings" by the French. No matter how many

The cathedral in Strasbourg, like hundreds of other French cathedrals and churches, sets up its traditional crèche a few days before Christmas.

This beautiful family crèche is from Vaucluse. Filippi, a Toulon santon maker, created the pieces around 1940. Each year, the painter Henri Pertus changes the background. The village used here is Saint-Martin-de-Castillon in Haute-Provence, where the family vacations.

crèche figures a family may already have, there is always room for more. New additions may be purchased each year to replace worn or broken ones, or to add a new dimension to the scene.

In the southern region of Provence, moss and pine boughs are needed, too, to use as background for the crèche. Children traditionally make a special trip to the woods and fields a few days before Christmas to find the materials. There they gather the moss and branches, plus handfuls of small stones—all for the crèche. Later, at home, the family will make the scene as real as possible. A length of deep-blue cloth may become a perfect nighttime sky; a small mirror may become a miniature lake.

Often, children will have made other items for the scene: cardboard farm buildings, a small papier-mâché bridge, or a hill or two. The tiny crèche figures are placed as realistically as possible. Villagers are either on their way to the manger or busy at their usual jobs: sawing wood, drawing water from the well, or perhaps sitting around a bubbling cauldron. Shepherds huddle around a minuscule fire made from red tin foil; the Three Kings seem to move closer to the manger as Christmas Eve approaches.

Once all the figures are arranged, moss, stones, or pine boughs are added for a final touch of authenticity. Fluffy snow for a winter scene is created with flour from the kitchen or with cotton. Finally the crèche is complete, except for one image: the tiny Infant Jesus. The manger remains empty until Christmas Eve, for it is not until then that the Christ Child will be born.

As the preparations for Noël progress, there are many community activities observed. Saint Nicholas Day on December 6 is eagerly anticipated by youngsters in many regions of France, for it means gifts of candy and other goodies.

Saint Nicholas really did exist. He was a bishop in Asia Minor who, it is believed, performed many miracles. He became the patron saint of sailors, scholars, clerks, bankers, and children. According to legend, Saint Nicholas once performed a miracle that brought three small boys back from death. A wicked, greedy innkeeper had murdered the children and placed their bodies in a barrel of brine. But the good saint brought them back to life.

Saint Nicholas is also the patron saint of Lorraine, a province of northeastern France. There his feast day is celebrated as a major festival. Each year processions wind through the old, narrow streets of the province's towns and villages, led by one or more men dressed up to represent the saint. The men carry crosses and wear tall, pointed bishops' hats. And behind them comes a cart, holding a barrel and images of the three rescued boys of legend.

There may also be another character walking in the procession. He is Père Fouettard, Father Whipper, an ugly, mean-spirited figure. Père Fouettard wears a long, dirty, dark-colored robe and a gray, poorly groomed beard.

Instead of a sack of goodies, Père Fouettard carries an armload of switches. Most children are not afraid of Père Fouettard, at least not when they are together in a group and can run after him, calling out insults. But it may be a different story at home, especially if a child has not been behaving well.

After all, as their parents occasionally remind them, Père Fouettard has been known to come into a house and drag bad children right out of bed for a spanking!

A holiday trip past the square next to the Beaubourg Museum in Paris may find street musicians entertaining the crowds there. Performing groups come to the square, too, such as Les Baladins, a band of mimes. *Les Baladins* means "the buffoons," and they are a charming lot, amusing onlookers with their silent pantomime routines. In between performances the actors sometimes stay around the square in their clownlike costumes and smiling painted faces, offering flowers to passers-by.

At the Cathedral of Notre Dame de Paris, the Nativity story is presented each year by regional groups from all over France. The city sponsors the performances, and admission is free. Men and women wear their native costumes and sing their traditional carols, many going back to the Middle Ages. Some shows may be simple choral presentations or carols mixed with regional dances. Others are modern interpretations of medieval Christmas plays, set to music. These performances, called *pastorales,* are loaded with local humor and are often sung or spoken in the performers' native dialects. Pastorales are performed today in many regions of France, in community theaters, concert halls, and churches.

Provence, particularly, specializes in Christmas Eve processions of shepherds who reenact the Nativity story with carols and music. Local townspeople act out the roles just as their forebearers did in medieval days. Live animals are sometimes a part of the proceedings, too: oxen, donkeys, horses, lambs, and sheep.

The processions are enormously popular, both among the local residents and the great numbers of tourists who flock to the area to see them. The spectacles frequently end with a living crèche, where townspeople represent the manger figures. Often a live lamb takes part and, in some cases, the Christ Child is portrayed by a real baby. They are charming, the living crèches—simple, and very moving.

French children have a two- or three-weeks' holiday from school at Christmastime. Some families go off to France's snowy regions for skiing, sledding, and tobogganing. A few head south to the warm Riviera. But there is plenty to do to keep everyone occupied right at home.

In addition to attending Christmas performances and generally decorating for the holiday, preparing for Noël in some parts of France also means cleaning the house to the peak of perfection. In former times, housewives scurried about in a frantic rush to have everything spotless by Christmas Eve.

In Sologne, in central France, the harried woman traditionally had to sweep the chimney. Then she swept the house, backwards, finishing up in front of the chimney. Then she scrubbed the tiles, and—finally—she baked and cooked.

Modern families go about the housework in a more leisurely way, but not much more. Dusting and waxing needs to be done. The family's finest china and silver must be brought out and polished to shining splendor for the Christmas meal.

There is baking to be done, too, along with all the other careful preparations for the holiday foods. The smells of good things to eat blend with the sharper odors of wax and furniture polish, and the piny scent of the Christmas tree to become the distinctive fragrance of Noël.

The Christmas season finds youngsters singing carols indoors around the crèche and out-of-doors with their friends. In the regions of France bordering West Germany and Switzerland, bemused onlookers find outdoor Christmas trees that put them in the holiday mood. The outdoor tree is not too common a sight in the rest of France, but other imaginative decorations are: practical arrangements that add color and spirit to the holiday scene.

Showing that very little really has to go to waste, one Christmas a Parisian flower shop presented a smiling styrofoam snowman at its door. The owners had saved the styrofoam day by day from packages received at the shop.

By invitation of the city of Paris, a regional group performs a Nativity play at Notre Dame.

These performers from Château-Gombert present a pastorale in Ollioules, Department of Var.

They patiently glued the unmanageable pieces together into two large white orbs, just like snowballs. Then they formed a smaller ball for the snowman's head, assembled the pieces, and added a black top hat, eyes, mouth, and a pipe. The snowman became their holiday doorman. Next to him, a sign read: WITHOUT FLOWERS, NO PRESENTS. With customers given this call to duty, perhaps business was unusually good for the flower shop that season. Still, there is one item that Christmas hunters will seek out more than anything else—toys!

Toy shopping is an exciting part of the pre-Christmas preparations. One toy manufacturer in Paris, Nain bleu, offers doll-sized sets of Limoges china. Toy farms, complete with buildings, cows, chickens, rabbits, a milkmaid, and a shepherd are sold at another shop, Train bleu.

For Christmas, the famed Galeries Lafayette in

Paris sometimes becomes a fairyland of tiny white lights, clustered like a vault of stars under protective outdoor marquees. Inside the department store, a marvelous village of toys is full of dolls, stuffed animals, trains, and all manner of tempting gifts—just for children.

The window scenes at the Galeries, the nearby Printemps, and other stores often include animated figures of animals and Christmas characters. Passing youngsters are fascinated by the figures' movements; so are most adults. There are Wild West displays with horses and cowboys, and popular spaceship scenes, village streets in miniature, and snowy vignettes complete with merry elves working busily, making Christmas toys. Dolls galore inhabit toy-shop windows; in one, a charming wrought-iron Ferris wheel revolved one year, a pair of dolls in each seat, one doll holding its own Teddy bear.

There are enchanting seasonal scenes for adults, too. Slinky, black-gowned mannequins, some adorned with gorgeous furs, may grace the windows of Dior, the famed dress designer. At Pierre Cardin, a novel display recently showed a bald male mannequin seated next to a large, clear plastic hippopotamus standing on two legs. The hippo was actually a table on which was placed a bottle of champagne in a silver bucket.

France is known not only for its superb champagne, but also for its perfumes. They, too, are displayed with matchless elegance. In the perfume department of the Galeries Lafayette, imposing arrays of exquisitely packaged scents may be found arranged under a great roof of twinkling white lights.

Delectable chocolates are another French specialty. Candy shops offer glorious displays of luscious sweets, unadorned or wrapped in rainbow shades of foil.

A delectable display might present the humble wooden shoe refashioned in dark chocolate and filled

On a rainy winter evening, white, glittering lights reflect against Paris' Boulevard Haussmann. Shoppers flock to see the window displays at the Printemps department store.

with little hard candies, each wrapped in crinkly colored paper. Also to be seen are great pyramids of foil-wrapped candies, presenting a challenge to the most persisting sweet tooth.

At night, the glittering lights of decorated streets reflect in the display windows of the shopping districts, doubling the radiance. Most streets in France have only tiny white lights to herald the winter holidays. There are strings of white, globes of white, bells of white, candles of white—all adding to the splendor of the season.

In the west of France, there is more color in the outdoor decorations. Large red candles are a favorite, made up of dozens of small electric lights and tipped with a flame of shining yellow.

But it would be a mistake to think that Christmas to the French is all glitter and glow. Though the shopping districts may sport a holiday costume, the home keeps its simple dress, and the daily routine goes on.

Children love the cowboy display at the Printemps department store (above right). *Here, Papa gives his little girl a boost so she can get a better look at the new types of toys Père Noël might bring this season* (below).

At the Galeries Lafayette, a vault of
fairy lights shines above the perfume
stalls, reminding shoppers that it is
time to purchase seasonal gifts for
grown-ups (above). In Toulon, a little
boy resists having his photograph
taken with a patient Père Noël
(right).

There are some who would insist, however, that the household atmosphere is a little more orderly, what with the children getting ready for Père Noël's visit.

The children of France, as those of many lands, are never sure until Christmas morning whether they have behaved well enough all year to deserve receiving gifts from the Christmas Spirit. Certainly, any French child with serious doubts will make a special effort to be polite and helpful as the big night approaches.

Most French children must also take care of one last, important detail. They write carefully composed letters to Père Noël. The youngsters are taught to speak with the utmost respect to adults, and the letters reflect their training. Père Noël will undoubtedly find this one irresistible:

Dear Père Noël,
My name is Régine Wargny and I live in Ville-
neuve on Fère près de Château-Thierry, in Aisne.
Since it will soon be Christmas, I am writing to
you to tell you that I would love for you to bring
me a big doll that talks and walks, with long blond
hair and a pretty dress, and also I would love some
chocolates. This year I have been very good and I
have worked well at school. I have never been pun-
ished. Christmas Eve, I will put my nice shoes and
some beet greens for your donkey to one side of
the fir tree.
I hope that it will not be too cold and that you
will not catch a cold while giving out the gifts. I
thank you for what you are going to send me.
Affectionately,
Régine

The letters are mailed to Père Noël at the North Pole. On the way to the mailbox, there is the possibility that some lucky children might actually see Père Noël himself! He does not appear in France as commonly as Santa does in the United States and Canada, but occasionally he may show up on a street corner or in a department store.

Once their letters to Père Noël are mailed, French children find it difficult to wait for Christmas Eve. The great night always comes, however, and youngsters' patience is well rewarded. Noël—what a time for the children of France.

Brother and sister go hand-in-hand to post their letter to Père Noël.

REVEILLON: THE HOLIDAY FEAST

The Christmas holiday in France is observed in many ways—and especially in the preparation of exquisite foods for children and adults. One of the grandest meals of the entire year is served at Christmas: the Christmas Eve "supper," called the *réveillon*. It is much more than just a simple supper, though. It is a lavish spread of delicious foods, course after course—all prepared in the fine tradition of French cooking.

The cuisine of France, renowned the world over, has come a long way since the days of Charlemagne, king of the Franks. In his time—the late 700's and early 800's—dinner was usually a large piece of meat or fish cooked on a spit. It was not until the 1300's that food in France began to receive any special treatment at all. When it did, dining (at least in the royal houses) became an occasion of magnificent splendor, notably at Christmastime.

Chefs vied with one another to serve spectacular dishes, including creations called *sotelties*. Made of pastry or spun sugar, they depicted miniature castles, Biblical scenes, or exotic birds and beasts.

French cuisine finally became an art in the late 1600's, during the reign of King Louis XIV. He employed more than 50 chefs and lesser kitchen helpers in his royal residence at Versailles. Some of France's fabulous sauces were introduced at Louis XIV's table, as were *pâtés*—meat spreads, frequently of liver—and other delicacies. And, instead of massive quantities of the indigestible, highly spiced foods from previous eras, smaller portions of exquisitely prepared meats or fish were offered.

Interest in superb cuisine has never lessened in France. Today, restaurants, large or small, serve marvelous food, and French housewives pride them-

Candy factories in France produce thousands of scrumptious holiday confections, including these foot-high chocolate Père Noëls (above). This candy shop shows nuts, dried and glazed fruits, and every kind of candy imaginable to a hopeful little girl (right).

A Parisian pastry maker proudly presents a bûche de Noël almost the size of a real log (above). To the south, in Provence, a Christmas Eve produce market is loaded with fruits for making some of the 13 Christmas desserts (left).

selves on their cooking. At Christmastime, they outdo themselves.

There is no one traditional réveillon dinner in France. The courses vary widely, according to the region. But whatever the locale, the meal will offer the very best of French cuisine.

To prepare for it, the French go shopping shortly before Christmas Eve. The task is not a matter of running into a supermarket and loading up a cart with packaged items. Shopping takes time and a good deal of effort, for only the highest quality foods—and the freshest—are acceptable.

In France, food is usually purchased over several days from individual shops or market stalls. The French housewife sets forth with her shopping cart or shopping bag of nylon netting to visit a long list of specialty shops.

She may begin at the fruit stalls. These are gorgeous sights with their colorful pyramids of offerings: oranges, apples, bananas, grapes, pears, tangerines, and plums. The French like their fruit very ripe, so that it may be peeled with a butter knife. The selection is a careful one.

The *boucherie*, or butcher shop, could come next. There, the shopper selects a roast of beef, a leg of lamb, or a plump goose, chicken, turkey, or duck. Exotic delicacies are wild boar or venison.

In the country, there are open-air fowl markets. The scene is a noisy one, with live geese and ducks waddling about loose or in pens, defiantly honking and quacking at passers-by. Ducks and geese already killed and plucked may hang stiffly in the background, sometimes on a string in two's or three's or more. Pheasants, still in their gorgeous plumage, tiny quails, and grouse may also be offered for sale.

Vendors in navy blue smocks and berets wait patiently for interested buyers or chat with friends. Sometimes an old dog lies dozing by the side of his master, peacefully ignoring all the commotion. Old women vendors, scarved and wrinkled, keep themselves occupied with their knitting.

Next, one might visit the *pâtisserie,* or pastry shop. The highlight of Christmas dinner in France is

There is something for everyone at the poultry market in Réalmont. Shoppers select their favorite réveillon bird from among turkeys, chickens, ducks, and geese.

25

the *bûche de Noël,* a cake shaped like a log. It is a latter-day, edible version of the ancient yule log. Pâtisseries offer all kinds of bûches, covered in dark or light chocolate, or even white chocolate tinted in many colors.

Basically the bûche is a sponge cake rolled with chocolate butter cream filling. Then it is frosted, and the brown icing is marked with lines, making it look just like real bark. Sometimes extra pieces of cake have been added under the frosting, in bumps like tree knots, for even more realism. Then the log is decorated with confectioners' sugar, nuts, little images of Père Noël, sugar roses or real roses, elves, or perhaps sprigs of fresh holly.

Serving a bûche de Noël is so traditional at Christmas that it sometimes even appears in other forms. Recipes are printed in French magazines each year suggesting substitutes, such as a bûche made of layers of puréed carrots, spinach, and other vegetables, jelled and molded into a log. Or, there is a bûche of chilled pâté, frosted with a layer of rendered fat.

Along with the bûches de Noël, most pastry shops offer luscious trays of *tartes,* or pies, tartlets, petits fours, napoleons, éclairs, and all the other delectable pastries devised by the French. Often there will be a special display showing off the pastry maker's skill— such as a sleigh with Père Noël inside—all made from pastry, chocolate, and icing.

Another shop on the list is the *poissonnerie,* the fish shop. Silvery rows of fish of all kinds are on display, captured from the seas or from freshwater streams and rivers. Next are shellfish: snails, sea urchins, shrimps, clams, and mussels. Lobster is a favorite choice for the réveillon. Oysters, too, are traditional in many families.

Pâtés in many varieties are an important part of the réveillon. They are often purchased at the *charcuterie,* a unique kind of shop offering not just pâtés but all manner of prepared foods to take home: roast chickens and salads, snails in garlicky breadcrumbs, glazed hams, and trout or salmon in aspic. Occasionally, in the window a whole piglet is on display, boned, stuffed, cooked, and sold by the slice.

Many people associate pâtés only with goose livers, but there are many kinds. Some are of rabbit or of duck mixed with minced ham or pork. They may appear *en croûte,* or baked in a shell of pastry. They are all to be eaten with bread and tiny sour pickles to complement the delicate flavor of the pâté.

Cheeses in all shapes, sizes, and smells are on sale at the charcuterie, too, and in other shops or stalls. A large disk of Camembert is a popular choice to take home and let sit until it is deliciously soft and runny.

For bread, one goes to the *boulangerie,* or bakery.

Christmas means seafood to diners all over France, as this decorated Parisian fish market shows. Available are many delights from the seas including oysters, sea urchins, shrimps, and clams.

Neat rows of truffles set off the dozens of pâtés and glazed birds in this charcuterie, a type of store that offers assorted prepared foods for the holiday feasting.

All is in readiness for the réveillon at this restaurant in Strasbourg.

The shopwindow and all the shelves are loaded with an awesome array of crusty loaves. There is the *baguette,* a long, narrow loaf, and smaller loaves called *pain de mie,* or bakery bread. Alongside are Italian-style loaves. Then come breads made with walnuts, raisins, or anise; egg breads; and countless other varieties. The largest of all is the startling *pain de campagne,* or country bread, sometimes 3 feet long and a foot wide.

If Maman has taken the children shopping, they may feel there is still one more shop to visit: the *confiserie,* or candy shop. Boxes of delicious chocolates and hard candies are on display in the window, on the shelves, and on tables. Nearby are candied fruits in a profusion of choices: cherries dipped in white frosting, sugary pineapple segments, pears, dates, and

apricots. It is almost impossible to make a decision—it all smells so good!

Stunning are the elegant food shops like Fauchon in Paris, in the Place de la Madeleine. Fauchon offers a wide range of exquisite foods. Those who can shop there may have an exotically decorated duck for their réveillon table.

But now all is done, the shopping is finally accomplished. It is time to go home. Christmas Eve—and the réveillon—are fast approaching.

27

NOELS FROM THE PAST

Christmas has been celebrated in France for almost 1,500 years. The religious observance is tied to important historical events. France was once part of an extensive region known as Gaul. The Romans conquered the area in the time of Julius Caesar, between 58 and 51 B.C., making Gaul a province of Rome. The Romans adopted Christianity in the 300's, and their legions carried it to France.

In the 400's, a non-Christian German tribe called the Franks took over much of Gaul. By the end of the century, Clovis, their king then, was a powerful ruler. He married a Christian princess of Burgundy named Clotilda, who persuaded him to convert to her faith. On Christmas Day in the year 496, Saint Rémi, bishop of Reims, baptized Clovis and 3,000 of his men. And France's first Christmas celebration was observed.

The fabled warrior Charlemagne (Charles the Great) became king of the Franks in 768. In 799, Pope Leo III was driven from Rome after being accused of crimes against the church. Charlemagne granted him refuge and later presided over a tribunal in Rome in which the pope was proved innocent. On

Christmas Day in the year 800, Pope Leo crowned Charlemagne emperor of the Romans. The splendid ceremony was held in the original Saint Peter's Church in Rome.

Christmas in medieval France was a glorious occasion, especially at court. It was customary for the castle gates to remain open all through Christmas Night. Strangers were made welcome in the great dining halls, and no one ever asked the travelers' names or destinations.

If a needy guest appeared, the *châtelaine,* or lady of the castle, would slip a loaf of bread, a bit of meat, and perhaps a few coins into his pouch. Sometimes

On Christmas Day, 800, Pope Leo III crowned Charlemagne Emperor of the Romans (above). The Franks became a Christian tribe on Christmas Day 496, when Saint Rémi baptized Clovis I, King of the Franks, and 3,000 of his men in the city of Reims (right).

he might even go away the next day with a new coat, leaving his tattered old garment behind.

Christmas in the castles was a jolly, noisy affair, with hundreds of guests enjoying vast amounts of food—and quantities of wine and other spirits. Huge logs burned merrily in the tall fireplaces; torches cast their dim, smoky light upon the revelers. The chilly stone floors were strewn with rushes, herbs, and sweet-smelling grasses. Tapestries on the walls helped—a little—to keep out the drafts.

Fantastic banquets were served by hordes of scurrying servants. Peacock was a favorite dish, as were swan and even stork. In Charlemagne's day, the cooking was done over open fires. Fingers were usually the only utensils, except for a knife or sword to cut the meat.

All sorts of entertainment accompanied the Christmas dinner: jugglers, magicians, dancers, masquerades. Outdoors there were often exciting jousting tournaments and wild boar hunts for the noble lords.

Though fun loving, the medieval French were at the same time pious. Kings and queens, lords and ladies, and the folk attended impressive Masses during the Christmas season. The lucky ones could enjoy services at one of the majestic new Gothic cathedrals such as Notre Dame in Chartres, which was constructed mainly during the 1200's.

Storytelling played an important role in the holiday celebrations, too, for both rich and poor. Traveling musicians sang and recited ancient legends in royal halls and in small villages—to enthralled audiences. They often sang of miracles that took place on Christmas Eve.

Devotion to the real reason for Christmas—Christ's birth—was shown in medieval France in other ways besides churchgoing and storytelling. One custom came from Italy.

In 1223, Saint Francis re-created the event of Christ's birth with a live Nativity scene in the hills near Assisi, Italy. The beloved saint arranged a touching scene—a manger filled with hay, with a real ox and donkey to watch over the Newborn Child and breathe warmth upon Him.

Legend says that the family of Saint Francis of Assisi brought the tradition of the crèche to France during the Middle Ages.

Saint Francis placed a wax image of Jesus into the humble crib and then related the Nativity story to the villagers and shepherds who had gathered to witness the unusual event. The people loved the idea and, before long, the charming manger scene was being re-created in other villages throughout Italy. Somewhere along the way, a notion of also using miniature figures to tell the story was conceived.

From Italy, the custom spread rapidly to other European countries. There were both the live manger scene and the one with small replicas of Joseph, Mary, the Babe, and all the other Biblical characters. In time, new participants, representing local types of diverse occupations, were added.

In France, the manger scene, or crèche, first appeared in Avignon sometime between 1316 and 1334. Legend says that members of Saint Francis' own family imported the tradition. The French people quickly adopted the idea, and over the years it became one of the more popular French Christmas customs. In Provence, artisans create the marvelous terra-cotta crèche figures called *santons*. The art form is unique to France, and the simple loveliness of the hand-painted figures is unmatched anywhere else in the world. Marseille is the home of the yearly santon fair, first held there in 1803.

Religious dramas called mystery or miracle plays also began to be performed in France during the Middle Ages. These plays were acted-out versions of the events surrounding Christ's life and the lives of the saints. Originally presented by the church, the dramas were devised to teach the Bible to the people, most of whom could not read or write. The earliest *noëls,* or French Christmas songs, appeared about that time, too.

At first the noëls were hymns, solemn melodies sung in Latin. A new sort of noël began to be heard in the 1400's. This form was sung in local dialects, often to the tunes of popular songs. Noëls of this period sometimes contained nonreligious verses. The songs were included in the rural shepherds' plays, the pastorales. The noëls were sung both as key parts of the scenes and also as links from one scene to another.

The carols were so well liked that whole collections of them, called *bibles de Noël,* were published between the 1500's and 1700's. By the beginning of the 1700's, French Christmas songs had become very gay and lively. In the 1800's, the noëls switched character once again and, reflecting the tone of the era, turned rather stiff and pompous.

Yet the most famous and beloved—though not most artistically admired—French noël of all was written during that period. It is the beautiful "Minuit, Chrétiens!" or "Oh, Holy Night." The words to the

The annual santon fair was first held in Marseille in 1803. It remains a popular holiday attraction today.

carol, now sung all over the world, were written by Placide Cappeau, the mayor of the small town of Roquemaure.

Cappeau's business was selling wine, and as he traveled from village to village he would amuse himself by making up verses. One day the curate of Roquemaure asked Monsieur Cappeau to write some verses for a Christmas carol. The curate wanted them for one of his congregation, a Madame Laurey, who had an especially fine voice.

On his next wine-selling journey, Monsieur Cappeau found the time to write the words to the poem he called "Minuit, Chrétiens!" Madame Laurey liked the poem and took it to her friend, the celebrated composer Adolphe Adam. He was ill at the time and, to distract himself, composed a melody for Cappeau's poem.

Madame Laurey sang the carol for the first time on Christmas Eve, 1847, in the little church of Roquemaure. It was an instant success. Later, the noted bar-

itone Jean-Baptiste Faure sang "Minuit, Chrétiens!" at midnight Mass in a church in Paris, and the lovely carol was on its way to world-wide fame. Today, all over France, church congregations traditionally sing the carol at the stroke of midnight on Christmas Eve.

Although the custom of the Christmas tree does not go so far back in French history as many other Christmas traditions, there are mentions of Christmas trees starting from the early 1600's. The area of their first appearance is Alsace-Lorraine, in the northeast, close to Germany.

The culture of Alsace-Lorraine has been part German and part French for many hundreds of years. Both countries waged wars for control of the region, and although it has been French since 1945, German customs are still practiced by many of its people. Putting up a Christmas tree is one of the customs that began in Alsace-Lorraine, later to spread westward.

In 1605, a traveler reported that the inhabitants of Strasbourg, on the German border, had fir trees in their homes at Christmas. The trees were, to his astonishment, adorned with paper roses, apples, candy, and sugary cookie wafers.

Paris was first introduced to the Christmas tree in 1837, when Princess Helen of Mecklenburg brought the charming notion with her to the city after her marriage to the Duke of Orléans. Emperor Napoleon III, in 1867, set one up for his small son in the gardens of his royal residence, the Tuileries.

Besides the Christmas tree, also from Alsace-Lorraine comes the legend of Hans Trapp and the young maiden, who represented the Christ Child. These two Christmas personalities were said to visit the children of Alsace-Lorraine on Christmas Eve.

The fearsome Hans Trapp was in charge of doling out punishment to those girls and boys who had not behaved well during the year. But the maiden interceded for the children. When they promised to behave better in the future, she led them to a Christmas tree loaded with presents, and their fear of Hans Trapp vanished.

A very old Christmas custom all over France was the burning of the yule log. A huge length of wood was cut and ceremoniously dragged into the house. The log was set aflame just as the family left for Christmas Eve services. In some areas, it was supposed to burn several hours, through the three consecutive Christmas Masses everyone had to attend. In other areas, attempts were made to keep the log burning even longer.

The log was believed to have magical powers. A shepherdess might have tapped it with her crook to ensure a good lambing season. Even the log's embers were magical—the more sparks they sent out, the better the harvest was going to be. No one ever dared sit on the log as it was being prepared for the hearth, of course. If someone did, it was believed he or she would be cursed with an attack of boils within two days.

Many homes nowadays do not have fireplaces, and the old-time custom of the yule log has for the most part disappeared in France. It is not forgotten, though. The bûche de Noël, the Christmas cake shaped like a yule log and covered with chocolate "bark," appears in bakeshops and homes throughout France each Christmas.

Besides Christmas, another French winter holiday with ancient origins is New Year's Day, the Jour de l'an. It goes back to ancient Rome, to the midwinter holiday called the *calends*.

This Latin word means the first day of the month. When the first of the month also was the first day of the New Year, Romans traditionally visited a grove dedicated to the goddess Strenna. There they cut branches that were taken back to the city and presented to the magistrates in the goddess' honor. Sometimes the greenery was used to decorate the home, too. In time, these "gifts" of branches were replaced by real presents. The branches, and the later gifts, were called *strennae* in Latin, after the name of the goddess.

In modern France adults exchange gifts on New Year's Day, reserving Christmas presents for the children alone. The New Year's gifts are known as *étrennes,* showing the connection to the Latin origin of the word.

As étrennes, adults exchange all sorts of gifts:

The holy maiden and Hans Trapp discover that one of the children has been a bad boy in this Alsatian engraving from 1858.

A profusion of delights to come in the New Year dazzles the characters in a fantasy toy palace engraved in 1843.

flowers, perfume, jewelry, and books. They may also give one another good-luck medallions of precious metals, minted at the Hôtel de la Monnaie in Paris. These medallions carry engraved wishes for the New Year, as well as proverbs to uplift the spirit as the months go by.

Children are doubly fortunate during the winter holidays in France. At Christmas, they receive toys, games, and candy. On New Year's, they receive gifts of money, to do with exactly as they please.

New Year's is also the time when the mail carrier, local tradespeople, and domestic help receive their annual gifts, usually money placed in envelopes. Tradespeople used to send their errand boys to visit preferred customers on New Year's Day, to offer compliments of the season and a small present. The baker might have sent some pastry, and the butcher, a chicken—anything representing the trade of the sender.

In some parts of France, there is an old superstition that one should never give a gift before receiving one. Stingy types, therefore, can escape very easily from the burden of generosity. One penny-pinching soul was immortalized on his tombstone for his lack of holiday spirit. The tombstone reads:

Here lies, below white marble,
The most miserly man in Rennes,
Who died the very last day of the year,
For fear of giving étrennes.

New Year's Day is a time for visiting friends and relatives. In past years, the visits were rather formal in nature. Monsieur and Madame, dressed in their finest clothes, would set out in the afternoon to call on as many acquaintances as possible—or to leave visiting cards. Sometimes the visits would be the only time in the whole year when people would see some of their friends.

Earlier in the day, visits would have been made to relatives' homes, with the children in tow, also dressed in a manner that would satisfy Grand-père and Grand-mère, or perhaps a starchy old aunt.

Just as at Christmas, the real highlight of New

Year's Day in France is an elaborate réveillon. It is usually given by the oldest member of the family, and all the relatives, young and old, are invited. The main course is often a plump roast chicken, stuffed with sausage and chestnuts.

In some areas, past custom was to serve the bird with 12 young partridges, 30 hard-boiled eggs, and 30 black truffles all around. This interesting arrangement symbolized the New Year: the chicken represented the year itself, the partridges the months, the eggs the days, and the truffles the nights.

Resembling American Halloween, New Year's Day in France has long been associated with begging. Street musicians or bands of children used to gather under windows to serenade a household, not always with a great deal of musical talent.

Their perseverance paid off, however, whenever the master of the house tossed out some money—perhaps to make them go away. The coins were always wrapped in paper, a practical custom ensuring the gifts would be easily spotted after falling on the cobblestones. It also prevented the coins from damaging a recipient, should they accidentally hit the singer on the head.

January 6, Epiphany, is the last day of the French winter holiday season. Epiphany, called the Jour des rois, the Day of Kings, commemorates the date when the Three Wise Men were believed to have arrived at the manger in Bethlehem. In France, Epiphany was, and still is, marked by the serving of a special cake: the *galette des rois,* or the cake of kings.

The cake is the highlight of a party attended by both children and adults. The galette is carried to the dining table with great ceremony and always cut so there is one more slice than there are guests. The extra piece is for any poor person who might come to the door.

The cake is baked with a single bean or tiny porcelain figure inside. Whoever finds the bean becomes ruler for the day, chooses a consort, and has the fun of ordering everyone about. Children, especially, enjoy the suspense—who will get the special slice to become monarch for the day? Often the cake is portioned ahead of time, so that Maman can be sure one of the children will find the prize. Tradition also has it that a child gives out the pieces, providing the favored little ones with a degree of rule themselves. No matter who the king or queen turns out to be, everyone has a marvelous time.

In the 1500's, King Francis I took his retinue to Romorantin for the holidays. News came to him that a courtier of the neighboring count had found the bean in the galette des rois and was thoroughly enjoying himself playing king. Francis, in high spir-

The child Phebe, sitting under the New Year's table, is ready to portion out the cake of kings in this detail from a fifteenth-century miniature.

its, took exception and challenged the count and his courtiers to a mock battle.

The two groups faced each other with a "prodigious quantity of snowballs, eggs, and apples." The story goes that during the heat of "battle," someone tossed a burning chunk of wood and hit Francis—by chance—on his royal head. The king received a fairly serious wound but refused to punish the offender. On the day of kings, odd behavior was excusable.

Throughout the hundreds of years of celebrating the winter holiday season, the only time festive observances were subdued in France was during the French Revolution, from 1789 to 1799. For that period, many French people tried to do away with celebrations linking the country with its monarchical past.

Carols were altered by substituting names of prominent political leaders for royal characters in the lyrics, such as the Three Kings. Church bells were melted down for their bronze to increase the national treasury, and religious services were banned on Christmas Day. The cake of kings, too, came under attack as a symbol of the royalty. It survived, however, for a while with a new name—the cake of equality.

CHRISTMAS EVE IN PARIS

Christmas Eve has come, and the beautiful city of Paris is alight. Along the Champs-Elysées, toward the Arc de Triomphe, tree branches are strung with white lights. The arches of the Pont des Invalides are curves of light, reflecting like silvery garlands in the black waters below. Fir trees at the base of the Eiffel Tower are adorned with lights and garlands, too.

There is an air of excitement everywhere as shoppers make last-minute purchases of gifts and food before going home. This is a very special night for the children of Paris. Soon, Père Noël will come, bringing gifts to place in the children's shoes.

Petit Jésus, or Little Jesus, once was believed to visit the children personally on Christmas Night. Later, in many parts of the country, the Christmas spirit was called Petit Noël, or Little Christmas. Today, most French children believe Jesus sends Père Noël, or Father Christmas, in His place.

Père Noël does not look like the American Santa Claus; he is not a plump elf who comes riding in a sleigh drawn by reindeer. Instead, he is tall and slender, an imposing old man with a white beard, wear-

ing a long red robe edged with fur. Sometimes he wears wooden shoes. He carries a sackful of toys and goodies, and a donkey often accompanies him to help with the heavy sack.

Père Noël does not say, "Ho, ho, ho!" as Santa Claus does, either. He cries, "Tralala, tralala, bouli, bouli, boulah!"

On Christmas Eve, French children place their shoes, slippers, or boots near the fireplace, if there is one. If not, the shoes are set near the Christmas tree or the crèche. Sometimes the youngsters are allowed to use Papa's shoes—or big brother's—because the footwear is so much larger and can hold more presents.

At the Arc de Triomphe, the combined glow from decorations, monument, and traffic along the Champs-Elysées produces a spectacle of lights for Christmas Eve in Paris (above). The Pont des Invalides is bright with light as the time for midnight Mass approaches (right).

Fir trees with lights and garlands compete for attention with the Eiffel Tower's looming framework.

And, now and then, in the true spirit of Christmas, a family will arrange for other children from the neighborhood to place their shoes at the family hearth. Père Noël's generosity does not become strained during the Christmas Eve rush.

Père Noël has an entire country to visit on Christmas Eve, and he gets a bit hungry during his travels. So, children often leave a little snack for him, and sometimes even a glass of wine. Thoughtful youngsters will also leave a bit of food for the donkey.

Late Christmas Eve, Père Noël will come, walking with his donkey. He will leave the animal outside the house and then come down the chimney. If there is no chimney, no matter; he will get in somehow—for Père Noël is magical.

As the children wait for Père Noël, Maman is finishing up her last-minute preparations for the réveillon to take place after midnight Mass. Usually a light snack of some sort is served before going to church because it will be a long time until the family returns for the big Christmas meal.

While Maman is putting on the final touches in the kitchen, the children often sing carols beside the crèche, to the delight of their parents and other relatives who may be enjoying Christmas Night with the family.

Older children or adults may tell Christmas stories to the little ones at this time, filling their minds with the wonder and merriment of the season.

The most famous French Christmas story and the most beloved to the people of France was published by Alphonse Daudet in the 1860's. Its title is "The Three Masses."

Daudet is said to be the French Charles Dickens. And the story of the three Masses is, at least in popularity, the French counterpart to *A Christmas Carol,* Dickens' story about Tiny Tim and the miser Ebenezer Scrooge.

But "The Three Masses" is unlike Dickens' story because it is not about someone who loves money. Instead, it is about people who love food. They love food so much, in fact, that on Christmas Eve they forget their devotion to God. Their punishment is a heavy one, and one that makes French children listening to the story think twice before misbehaving in any way on holy Christmas Night.

The story has a historical basis. For many hundreds of years, three consecutive Masses were celebrated on Christmas Eve in the churches and cathedrals of France. The worshipers became so hungry from having to sit through so many hours of devotions that, when they arrived home, they were famished. That was how the réveillon began: everyone was in the mood for a tremendous meal after Mass. And sometimes they were ready for it even before the Masses began.

According to Daudet, such was the state of Father Balaguère one Christmas Eve, just before midnight, when he was speaking to his altar boy, Garrigou:

"Two turkeys, Garrigou?" he asked.

"Yes, Your Reverence," the boy replied. "Two magnificent turkeys. They're so fat, their skin is stretched to groaning. And there are many other good things, too: plump, juicy trout, and quail and wine, and . . ."

"Enough, Garrigou!" the priest stopped the boy. "Quickly, help me dress for the services. For it is Christmas Eve, and we must not think only of food. Light the candles and ring the bell for the start of the first Mass. Hurry!"

In truth, Garrigou the altar boy was not what he seemed. The Devil, on this night, had crept into the boy in order to lure Father Balaguère into the sin of gluttony, or greedy eating. And, even as the Mass began, the good priest's thoughts were on Garrigou's descriptions of the food to come, not on the prayers of the Mass.

It is late Christmas Eve. The time has finally come to put Little Jesus into the family crèche.

During the night, Père Noël will leave presents at the fireplace for good girls and boys.

Garrigou rang his little bell, a tinkly sound. To Father Balaguère it seemed as though the bell was speaking. "Let's get going," it seemed to say. "The sooner we finish, the sooner we'll get to eat!"

That time and every time the bell rang afterward, the good priest forgot the Mass. He thought of the kitchen, the platters of food—those turkeys with their stuffing—oh, delight!

Somehow he managed to get through the first Mass, and he started on the second. The bell rang: "Ting-a-ling-ling, ting-a-ling-ling!" To Father Balaguère it said, "Quick, quick, let's get going!" And this time the priest raced through the Mass, speaking as rapidly as he possibly could. Garrigou (still with the Devil inside him) jabbered away just as fast with his responses at the altar.

"Two down!" the priest sighed as the second

Mass came to an end. And without taking a breath he plunged into the third Mass.

"Ting-a-ling-ling, ting-a-ling-ling," the bell rang again. Father Balaguère was lost. He skipped some verses, he did not finish others, and he completely forgot the Lord's Prayer. He simply hurled himself through the final Mass.

The congregation was startled at first, and a bit frightened. What was wrong with Father Balaguère? Some of the people stood when they should have been kneeling; others knelt when they should have been standing. The mass was turning into total confusion. But no one objected; the congregation wanted to go home for the réveillon, too.

Quickly the third Mass came to an end, and Father Balaguère wasted no time reaching the dining room. And he ate. And ate. And ate. He ate so much that,

The renowned organ music and choirs of Notre Dame draw people of many faiths to share the midnight Mass.

during the night, he suffered a dreadful attack of indigestion and died.

The next morning Father Balaguère arrived in heaven. God was exceedingly angry and said:

"You stole the Christmas Masses from Me, and you will pay three hundred times for your sin. You will not be allowed to enter paradise until you have celebrated three hundred full Christmas Eve Masses in your own chapel. And that goes for all your congregation, who sinned with you."

So, the story goes, on Christmas Eve the old chapel of Father Balaguère—lying now in ruins on the lands of Trinquilage—seems to come to life once again. Mysterious candles flicker, and the murmurs of distant voices may be heard. Some people believe that Father Balaguère himself, Garrigou, and the entire congregation are celebrating the Christmas Masses. And, perhaps, getting close to number 300!

Maman has finished her preparations. Now comes the moment the youngsters have been waiting for ever since they helped set up the crèche a few days before. It is time to place Little Jesus in His crib. The moment is very solemn.

Maman hands the tiny image to one of the children, perhaps the youngest, who very carefully takes it and approaches the crèche. Gently the Babe is laid into the miniature manger. The figures of Mary and Joseph look on with pride, and the Three Wise Men, all the shepherds, angels, and other figures do, too. The children say a little prayer to the newly born Christ Child, and the pretty ceremony is done.

Although older French children often accompany their parents to midnight Mass, the younger ones usually do not. They are tucked into bed to dream like youngsters everywhere of the presents to come in the morning. As soon as the children are safely asleep, Maman and Papa add the final touches to the Christmas tree: candies, fruit, and small toys snuggled into the branches. Then it is time to set off for church.

People of many faiths attend the Catholic Masses held in France's beautiful cathedrals and churches, some of which are several hundred years old. The glorious midnight Masses are more than just church services—they are cultural events.

There are more than 300 churches in Paris alone. Many, including the Church of Saint-Eustache and the Cathedral of Notre Dame de Paris, are renowned for their splendid Christmas Eve music. At Notre Dame the crowds are enormous, and the traffic around the cathedral virtually comes to a halt around the time of the Mass.

One year, the traffic was so tangled at Notre Dame that a cardinal, not wishing to be late in arriving for midnight Mass, left his limousine where it was trapped in a solid line of cars and walked the rest of the way. As he reached the cathedral, some children waiting in the crowd saw his red garb and thought he was Père Noël. The cardinal's entry into the cathedral was delayed for several more minutes, while he explained his true identity.

At Saint-Eustache Cathedral in Paris, a symphony accompanies the soloist, choir, and congregation on Christmas Eve as they sing a traditional noël (left). The Eiffel Tower is a tree of lights as Parisians return home for the réveillon (above).

On a tablecloth of heirloom lace, a Parisian hostess serves oysters as the first réveillon course.

Inside, magnificent Notre Dame is packed with people every year. Most are wearing somber clothing of blues and browns; the priests are all in white.

The Mass is celebrated under the massive Gothic arches of the cathedral, begun in 1163. Simple flower arrangements decorate the altars. Wisps of smoke curl up from the many, many flickering candles. Music from the mighty organ swells and ebbs, and the people of Paris lift their voices in song.

Saint-Eustache lures Parisians with its symphony and choirs of both adults and children. And some Parisians at Christmastime will make a traditional pilgrimage all the way to Chartres, known as France's Christmas cathedral, perhaps to hear the beautiful voices of a special group called the Petits chanteurs de la croix de bois, or the little singers of the wooden cross. They are the French counterpart of the Vienna Boys' Choir.

At the conclusion of the Mass the bells ring out, and Christmas is joyously welcomed in. Heading home, the people can see the Eiffel Tower shining forth, a Christmas tree of white lights almost a thousand feet tall. The moment of the réveillon has come.

Réveillon means "awakening." The Christmas Eve meal is enjoyed with all the gusto of New Year's in America. Restaurants in Paris remain open on Christmas Eve, for some people prefer to dine out this night. Most, however, make their way home from Mass for their own private réveillon. Families invite relatives and friends to share the Christmas meal; often large numbers of guests accept the invitation. And the réveillon can last all night.

The meal is tackled with high spirits and a sharp appetite. It is a happy, warm time of sharing, enjoying marvelous foods, and offering countless toasts with France's fine wines. The table is set with candles and a lovely cloth, perhaps an heirloom of Breton or Alençon lace. Maman and the female relatives or guests take care of all food preparations.

Throughout the lengthy meal, Maman never seems to sit still. She is up and down from the table, serving a course, eating what she can, and then jumping up to prepare and serve the next course. And there may be as many as 15 courses. For Maman, however, serving the réveillon is a labor of love.

Papa is in charge of the wine, and, as many different kinds may be served, his duty is a matter of some importance. Not only does he pour the wine but he must taste it first. It is always possible that a bottle will come from a bad batch or that the wine will have turned to vinegar. So Papa uncorks the bottle with great ceremony. Then he sniffs the cork, pours a bit of wine into his own glass, and tastes it. If all is well, then and only then will he fill his guests' glasses.

In Paris, the réveillon frequently begins with delectable oysters on the half shell. Then may come canapés and hors d'oeuvres, plus *pâté de foie gras,* or goose liver pâté—a favorite among many French families. A plump, golden-brown turkey could follow, or perhaps a goose stuffed with prunes and pâté. Whatever the bird, it is surrounded by all the trimmings: potatoes, peas, salad. No family favorite is left out.

Later there will be cheeses—perhaps Camembert, Brie, and Boursin. The more kinds, the better. And bread with sweet butter is always served in great quantity. Fruit is never left out, and neither are nuts: walnuts, pecans—all kinds. And, finally, Maman brings in the special Christmas cake: the rich, delicious bûche de Noël.

Each course may be accompanied by an appropriate wine, but some families provide a special treat: champagne, all the way through. At last, coffee is served, plus brandy and other liqueurs.

At this point, some families will open their presents. But parents with little children try to sneak in a few hours' sleep towards dawn of Christmas morning. They need it—for when the little ones emerge, sleepy-eyed and tousled, they are in a grand state of excitement. Père Noël has come!

The shoes left empty the night before are now hidden beneath piles of brightly wrapped gifts. And the snack for Père Noël is gone. Only a few crumbs remain. His glass of wine is empty, too. Even the treat left for the donkey has disappeared, to the youngsters' great joy.

Maman and Papa, worn out from the réveillon, sip coffee and watch while the children tear open their presents: dolls, trucks or racing cars, a stuffed animal or two, records, books and games. And sweets—perhaps a chocolate wooden shoe or Père Noël.

The grown-ups' celebration is yet to come. They will exchange their gifts on New Year's Day. But for the youngsters, Christmas is the big day, indeed. Père Noël has read their letters carefully. Somehow—with the help of loving parents?—he has managed to bring exactly the right gifts. The children of Paris have had a glorious Noël.

The réveillon complete, a family settles down to some strong black coffee and the opening of presents.

NOEL IN THE PROVINCES

France is a country of ancient provinces that were once individually ruled by kings, princes, and lesser nobility. In the late eighteenth century, the despised Bourbon monarchy was overthrown during the French Revolution. The provinces were abolished in 1790, and a new constitution was signed in 1791. The country was then divided into departments, each named for a mountain or stream.

Nearly 200 years have passed since the change from provinces to departments was made. Yet, even today a citizen of Nice, in the province of Provence, thinks of himself as a Provençal rather than as belonging to the department of the Maritime Alps. The old ways are still cherished—especially the old ways of celebrating Christmas.

Over the centuries, French Christmas has become an intricately woven tapestry of customs. Many regions share the same traditions; others have developed distinctly different ones. And some regions share their customs with Germany, Spain, and Italy—three countries that border France.

The Christmas climate varies, too, from the crisp, cold air and snow-clad slopes of the mountain regions to the semitropical warmth of the Mediterranean coast. In between are more temperate areas: rolling plains, a great central plateau, and the fertile valleys where grapes for France's wines are grown.

Many French families spend at least some of the Christmas holidays skiing, so ski resorts do a brisk business at this time of year. The French Alps are especially popular for winter vacationing. Even the younger members of the family zoom happily down the steep slopes, sometimes taking a tumble into the soft drifts. It is also fun to take a sleigh ride.

The horses' hoofs make a squeaking noise as they trot through the snow along narrow streets or head out into open countryside. The runners of the sleigh glide so effortlessly—the ride is almost like flying.

The air is nippy cold, but everyone is bundled up in warm coats and scarves. Children's cheeks burn rosy

People vacationing in the French Alps during the winter holidays may be treated to a ride in a genuine antique sleigh (above).

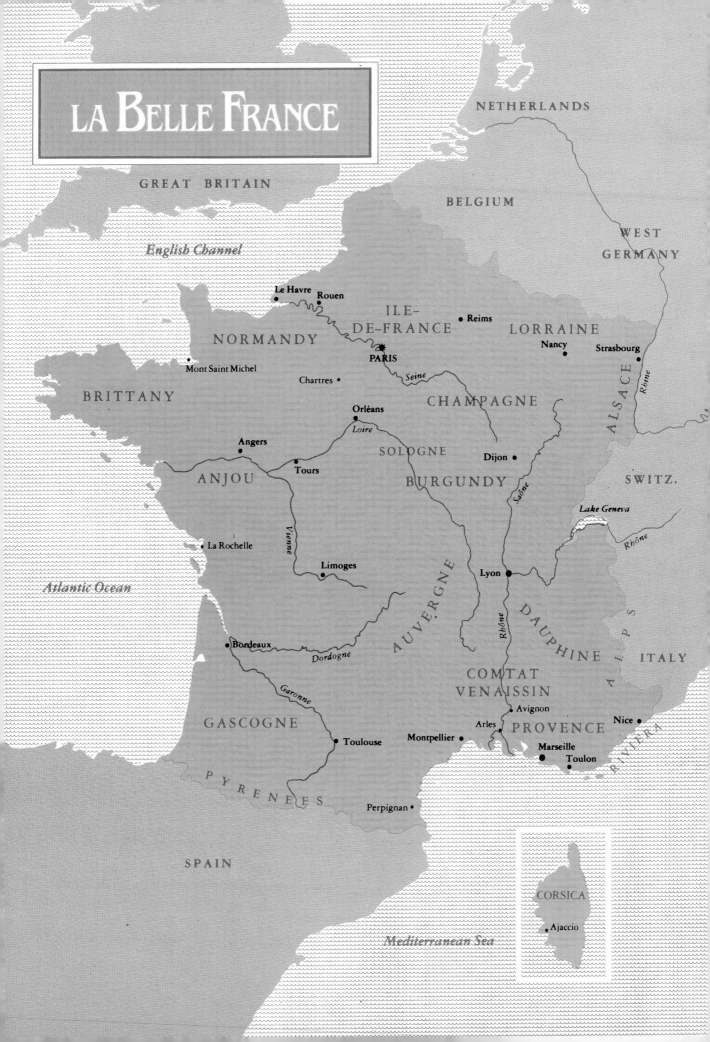

In Christmas greeting, a French girl places holly in the window of her alpine home.

red; their eyes sparkle with pleasure. Even the horses seem to enjoy the trip, snorting out clouds of steamy breath as they prance along, sleigh bells jingling.

The alpine scene is as Christmas-like as anyone could ask. Snowflakes drift lazily down, the branches of fir trees droop with their white burden. In the background and all around are massive mountains. They are awesome, these ranges, especially in the wintertime when they are covered with a deep, deep layer of snow and ice.

The small mountain villages look just like Christmas cards. In the town square, a tall Christmas tree may stand, aglitter with lights and ornaments. More holiday decorations hang suspended on wires over the village streets. And many homes have their own Christmas tree. Shiny green branches of red-berried holly may be seen through the windows, and usually some mistletoe, too. At night the stars twinkle frostily in the blue black sky. Rustic chapels, all alight, cast a glow of golden warmth across the snow.

The old province of Dauphiné in the French Alps is a cold, almost bleak mountain region. Icy ridges stretch for almost one hundred square miles. Secret, hidden valleys lie below, shadowed by the snowbound crests. The tops of these mountains are capped with snow the year round.

Bustling ski resorts have sprung up in the French Alps in recent years. But some parts of Dauphiné are still very much isolated during the winter. Sometimes so much snow falls that it forms a vault between the roofs of the houses. The people of one area, Oisans, share a special kind of kinship that comes from battling the elements together, year after year.

Life in the villages of Oisans has always been difficult, but the hardships have eased up recently. Nowadays, most houses have modern heating systems, for one thing. At one time, however, the cold was so bitter and heating supplies so precious that a whole village would gather in a single stable for warmth and light in the evenings. This custom was born of necessity, and it was one that also brought entire communities, animals included, together for feasts like the réveillon.

Christmas Eve has always been a special time for the people of Oisans. Even the animals in the stables receive extra food as a holiday treat. One old legend says that the animals kneel at the stroke of midnight in honor of the Infant Jesus. Another says that the statues of the saints in the chapels leave their niches at midnight on Christmas Eve to worship the Christ Child at the crèche.

In winter, light takes on a special meaning in this dark and frigid mountain region. The days are so short, and the nights so very long. Springtime seems far away. In some villages, the sun disappears completely for several months, hidden by the towering mountain peaks. Only a haunting gloom remains to light the steps of the alpine villagers.

In earlier times, people were not always certain that spring—and the shining sun—would ever come back again. So, they lighted great bonfires—called "fires of joy"—as celebrations of hope. Even today, in the community of d'Auris Station, a modern Christmas custom honors the power of light. Skiers, holding flaming torches, weave their way down the steep slopes, making a brilliant pattern of light against the darkness.

In the villages, the townsfolk light up the night of Christmas Eve with lanterns. Streets are dotted with small, moving lights as people scurry toward their chapels for midnight Mass. The services are simple and solemn, with flickering candles and old, traditional carols.

Midnight comes, and, with it, Christmas in the Alps. Once the Mass is done, out of the chapel come the villagers, heading homeward through the silent night. "Noël, Noël!" they call to one another as the church bells echo the sound. It is time for the réveillon, the Christmas feast.

In this frozen region, the foods are plain—not at all like the fancy fare of Paris and other large cities. The meal starts with a large bowl of hot soup, much appreciated after the walk through the cold outdoors. The soup is a bouillon, or clear broth, with *luzans,* a kind of pasta cut into diamond shapes. Then come *ravioles,* or stuffed pasta squares.

The main course may be a platter of boiled beef, or an omelet served with *escargots,* or snails. Even the omelet was once a traditional offering to the sun, in hopes the sun would soon reappear. For dessert, there is an enormous tarte, a delicious pie filled with prunes, pears, or squash.

In the old days, when the réveillon was held in the stable, the tablecloth would be carefully folded up over any remaining food and left there. Then, it was said, the Christmas angels coming to visit would be able to enjoy a Christmas snack themselves.

New Year's Day had its traditions, too, in the Alps. Housewives saved their best flour to make a loaf of white bread, the only one of the year and a great treat. The loaf was called the *chalanda.* And branches of juniper were burned in front of the houses to ensure prosperity in the coming year.

In southern France, near Spain, the people of Perpignan observe a mixture of both French and Spanish traditions. They speak Catalan, the local dialect. Here in the Pyrenees mountains, children eagerly await their presents on January 6, not on Christmas. And the gifts are brought not by Père Noël but by the Three Wise Men.

La Rochelle, on the Atlantic coast, is an old, historical port city, far away from the mountain peaks.

A rustic alpine chapel beckons warmly in Meribel, where worshipers must face frigid winds to attend midnight Mass (above). Down the icy slopes of d'Auris-Station, skiers welcome the birth of Christ with a torchlight procession (below).

To a stable in mountainous l'Oisans, revelers once hoped that the Christmas angels would come to enjoy food left on the réveillon table.

Cobblestone streets, medieval towers, and fishing boats create the backdrop for Noël by the sea.

In December, a click-clack, click-clack is mixed with the sounds coming from the docks. For, at Christmastime, La Rochelle turns its streets festive with a live Père Noël, dressed in his red gown and sporting wooden shoes.

The Père Noël of La Rochelle is a merry, white-bearded sign of Christmas. His gifts are hidden not in a sack, but in a basket strapped to his back. He tempts children of all ages to come see what Christmas joy he has brought with him to the seaside.

Farther to the north, this time on the English Channel, is the Mont Saint Michel. It is a large rock that juts from the foggy waters of Mont Saint Michel Bay, in Normandy. At the top of the rock are a medieval abbey and town.

The abbey of Mont Saint Michel is the site of Christmas pilgrimages. Hardy Normans and not-so-hardy tourists wishing to attend Mass there follow the priests and dignitaries up the winding streets of the town, then up hundreds of stairs, until they finally reach the abbey.

After services in nearby Brittany, Bretons may sit down to a traditional réveillon of buckwheat cakes and rich cream. The talk will likely be about the sea at one point or another, for there are many fine seaports with deep harbors in Brittany. Many Bretons become sailors or fishermen, and a rich folklore has developed about the sea. One popular story tells about the *ange de la mer,* the angel of the sea, who appears each Christmas Eve. A great white wing with feathers edged in black represents the angel. The wing guides ships lost at sea to safety on Christmas Night.

Another well-known Christmas legend from Brittany also has to do with a winged messenger, but this one appears to children, not to sailors. It is Jean Rouge-Gorge, or John Red-Throat, a tiny bird who happened to be in Bethlehem the night Jesus was born. John, present at the stable, noticed whenever Mary was becoming weary of tending Little Jesus. The bird would sing Jesus lullabies at these times, putting the Holy Child to sleep.

In La Rochelle, on the west coast of France, a boy cannot resist a childlike peek into Père Noël's basket (left). Garbed in native costumes, the youth of Arles sing out traditional noëls (above).

Later, when Jesus carried the cross and wore a crown of thorns, the bird appeared again. He sang the best he could, trying to ease Jesus' agony. A thorn pricked Jesus' head, and John plucked it out. As he did so, a drop of Jesus' blood touched the bird's small throat—and so he received the name Red-Throat.

When Jesus breathed His last breath, John flew quickly to gather it up, and then the little bird carried the breath straight to heaven. For this act of kindness, God allowed John Red-Throat to live on earth forever. And each year at Christmas, he searches for the most unhappy child he can find and grants the child a wish.

With all respect for the rest of France, the people of Provence, in the southeast, claim that nowhere else in the country is Christmas more devoutly observed. Certainly the Provençals celebrate the season with a great deal of exuberance. They have been enjoying Christmas in their own special way for centuries.

Provence's climate and its rugged terrain are somewhat similar to those of ancient Judea. Centuries ago, some inhabitants of the region believed that Jesus was really born in Provence, not in faraway Bethlehem, and that Provençal shepherds were the first to hear the news of Christ's birth.

Provence has its own Christmas dance, called the *farandole*. Legend has it that, after hearing the news that Christ was born, the shepherds, shepherdesses, and townspeople of Provence made up the dance on the way to see the Holy Child—in Bethlehem-en-Provence, of course.

One must remember, however, that Provence is not the only area of France that has claimed to be the birthplace of the Holy Child. Auvergne, in the mountains of south-central France, and also Brittany are two other regions with the same legend.

Still, the splendor of Christmas in Provence is hard to match. One knows the joyful season is coming when community groups begin to present Provençal carols at community gatherings. The singers wear native costumes dating back centuries.

49

During the midnight Mass, children form a living crèche at the church in Solliesville. In this town, a real baby plays the part of Little Jesus (above). Also in Provence, shepherds end their Christmas procession by bringing a live lamb to their church's crèche (right).

During the Middle Ages, the people in this region began a custom that has lost none of its popularity. On Christmas Eve, many Provençal villages reenact the story of the Nativity with a grand procession of shepherds and pilgrims. Frequently the procession ends with a living crèche.

The tradition probably began as a pageant staged in a local castle, acted out by the noble lords and ladies to entertain their guests. In later years, the townspeople adopted the custom for themselves, in a simpler, more meaningful way.

Near the ancient town of Les Baux, the annual procession moves toward the tiny church of Saint Vincent, founded in the Middle Ages. Les Baux is situated on a craggy, windswept plateau high above flat marshes. There are only a few dozen villagers in Les Baux, living among the ruins of a medieval fortress and town that flourished in the Middle Ages. The community of 4,000 people was devastated twice, then wrecked forever by gunpowder. Today, it is a veritable ghost town, with the remains of its castle looming precariously over the ruins.

At night, when the ruins are floodlighted, it is easy to imagine the castle as it once was. The visitor can almost see grand entourages of kings and popes, or knights in silvery armor clattering their way along the cobbled streets.

The story of Les Baux began with a legendary ruler named Balcio, or Balthasar. He, it is said, was descended from the legendary Balthasar, who was one of the Three Wise Men. Balcio came to the area at the time of the Roman occupation. His descendants built their massive fortress on a table of rock which they named Les Baux, after the Provençal word baou, or rock.

The coat of arms the feudal lords adopted is embellished with a many-rayed star; the people of Les Baux call it the Christmas Star, the star that led Balthasar and his companions to the Christ Child.

The lords of Les Baux were mighty, and very proud in medieval times. Their fortress was the seat of one of the more powerful and ancient feudal homes in Provence. These nobles were masters of more than 70 towns and villages between the Alps and the sea.

It was King Louis XIII, tired of resistance to his rule from the lords of Les Baux, who ordered the castle destroyed beyond repair in 1632. The area was given to the Prince of Monaco, whose land it has remained ever since. The new rulers partially rebuilt the fortress over the years, but during the French Revolution it was gutted by fire.

In later years the village on the rock became a haven for artists and writers, and the villagers have become known for their fine, handcrafted woodcarv-ings, pottery, and jewelry. And Les Baux became well-known for its Christmas Eve procession, called the "Fête de pâtrage."

The procession begins about an hour before midnight. Hundreds of participants patiently wait for the signal to light their candles. Then, like a curving ribbon of flame in the darkness, the figures slowly make their way towards the church.

All the characters of the original Nativity story are there—Joseph and Mary, angels of all sizes, the Three Kings, attired in gorgeous robes, and a host of shepherds and shepherdesses, all wearing their traditional brown woolen cloaks. Behind them come pilgrims from throughout the region, dressed in colorful regional costumes.

The ceremony begins as the procession enters the church. The choir softly sings an old Provençal carol, accompanied by shepherds playing galoubets, or fifes, and tambourins, the long, narrow drums of the region. Joseph, Mary, and the angels take their places at a living crèche set in a tiny chapel near the altar. The rest of the procession waits.

The priest appears and the Mass begins. At the Offertory—the part of the Mass when the parishioners bring the wine and the bread to the altar—the chief shepherd strides up the aisle. He leads a handsome, beribboned ram. It is pulling a small wooden cart, decorated with greenery, ribbons, and lighted candles. Inside the cart, a tiny lamb lies on a soft bed of moss.

Mary hands the priest a wax image of Little Jesus, and the priest holds the Infant high to show the congregation. Then the priest sits, still holding the Child, as the shepherds come one by one to bow and kiss the feet of the little image.

The lead shepherd now picks up the lamb and offers him to Jesus. The Three Kings move forward to present their gifts, too. And the shepherds come, each with a simple gift of honey or cheese, a live piglet, or a soft toy lamb. The Mass continues.

Just at the moment when the priest lifts the Host and chalice and the altar boys ring their tinkly bells, a shepherd tweaks the lamb's tail. It bleats, just like the cries of the Christ Child.

This organ in the church of Sollies-ville is the oldest in France, dating to 1499. With the assistance of a youthful helper, the organist is playing the antique instrument for the midnight Mass.

The drums roll—it is midnight! The choir and congregation joyously sing "Minuit, Chrétiens!" "Oh, Holy Night." The lamb is passed from shepherd to shepherd. Each one in turn bows to the Christ Child. Finally, the Mass ends, and the church empties to the cries of "Joyeux Noël!"

The Provençal town of Séguret also has a spectacular Christmas Eve procession, this time to the church of Saint-Denis. A huge, brilliant star is placed each year on a crag overlooking the village, to lead pilgrims from afar. The ceremony is called the "Bergie de Séguret," and the townspeople rehearse their roles for months in advance.

In Solliesville, another small town of Provence, the Christmas Eve celebration begins with an unusual ceremony. The entire village gathers at the town hall, where the mayor, imposing in his tricolored sash, makes a speech. Twelve village children stand waiting across a table. They are dressed in white vestments and represent the twelve apostles. When the mayor's speech is done, he hands each child a small gift, called an *obole.*

The custom began many years ago, when two local brothers distributed flour to all the town's needy at Christmastime. Now the gifts are presented to children. And, instead of bread, the oboles are much more appealing: chocolate bars and fruit, for instance. Real loaves of bread are handed out to the audience, however, preserving the tradition in full. Later, the town's dignitaries hold a festive supper.

On arriving at the church in Solliesville, parishioners will see a living crèche, with children representing the manger figures. This crèche has a special feature: a live baby plays the part of Little Jesus. The custom of having a live Christ Child for the crèche was once fairly widespread in Provence. In recent times, however, there are few towns that have kept this old tradition.

Solliesville has another important token from the past, one that fills its church full of Christmas gladness each year. The organ in the church of Solliesville is the oldest in France, dating from 1499. The antique instrument has provided music for midnight Mass for almost 500 years.

The Provençal Christmas celebration, with its bustle of processions, life-sized crèches, and costumed choirs, is a delight to see. But there is one part of Christmas there that is best enjoyed by a quiet fire, far away from the spectacle, where the children wait. This part is the telling of "The Réveillon of Piboule." The story is an ancient Provençal Christmas legend. It goes something like this:

Once there was a man named Piboule. He was terribly poor, not very healthy, and, in addition, was out of work. He was also bald and toothless. Piboule did, however, own a small piece of land—barren, of course. But he was content. He had his bit of soil and his tiny, rundown hovel of a house. All he asked was that God always allow him to keep his few, meager possessions.

Then one year, just before Christmas, a bear escaped from a traveling circus near Piboule's home. The owner offered a grand reward of 300 francs to anyone who could kill the dangerous animal. Piboule decided that he would try. He certainly could use the money.

So he took up his old, rusty gun and set off. Needing ammunition, he even spent his last few pennies for bullets. He hunted far and wide for two whole days and nights. But poor Piboule; he simply could not find that bear.

Then it was Christmas Eve. Piboule, tired, cold, and hungry, returned to his house. His spirits were very low. It was the night for the réveillon, but all he could find to eat was one solitary onion.

Always optimistic, Piboule ate it—with difficulty, since he had no teeth. Then he sent a prayer to God: "I am penniless, and I need that reward money. I did not get the bear: I could not find it. Do You think that You could possibly send the bear here—to my humble home—so that I could get the reward? If that is too much to ask, Lord, perhaps You could ask Little Jesus to leave some little thing for me by the fireplace. I will put my wooden shoes there for Him to fill, just in case." And, doing so, Piboule fell asleep on the thin mattress near the dying fire.

God must have been listening, for at the very stroke of midnight, Little Jesus came down the chimney. He placed a pot of honey in one of Piboule's shoes.

Now, everyone knows that bears love honey. Before long, the missing beast came sniffing, sniffing, from wherever he had been hiding. Finding Piboule's door open just a crack, the huge beast pushed his way inside. Just then, Piboule awoke with a start. Wonders! There was the bear and a present. His prayer had been answered—all of it.

Grabbing his gun, Piboule took careful aim at the bear. But the gun refused to fire. It was just too old, like Piboule. Thinking quickly, he picked up the pot of honey and ran from the house. The bear followed—right to Piboule's rickety stable. Piboule slammed the door shut and barred it.

During midnight Mass in Vaucluse, the faithful take Communion while a costumed choir sings noëls in a life-sized crèche setting.

Réveillon in southern France usually means plenty of lobster for everyone.

The next day, the circus owner heard that his bear had been raising a ruckus at the home of one Piboule, who had spared the animal's life. The owner hurried to Piboule's to find the bear at last. He was so glad to have the animal back alive, he gave Piboule the reward. And, so, the story ends happily for everyone—especially the bear.

Réveillon in Provence may begin with a clear broth, often of pheasant. Roast pheasant may appear as the main course, too, as may lamb, wrapped in a crust. But when one thinks of réveillon in Provence, the dish that springs to mind first is lobster—piles of the delicious shellfish, boiled to sweet perfection.

Served along with crusty loaves of bread are green salads, cheeses, pâtés, and several wines. And, not one—but 13—desserts.

The 13 desserts are an ancient custom, symbolizing Christ and the twelve apostles. Sometimes the delicacies are served heaped in glazed pottery bowls. Families also present the desserts more formally, carefully arranged on silver platters that grace the buffet.

There might be marzipan, nuts of all kinds, dark and light nougat, dried figs and dates, preserves, glazed fruit, and fresh fruit—oranges, winter pears, grapes, and apples. And cakes—a favorite is the *galette de Noël,* which is a flat, deep-fried disk dusted with sugar and dipped into warm honey. Another possibility is the *fougasse,* a sweet, buttery bread with cinnamon and sometimes anise. The fougasse is also served at Epiphany by some families.

A Provençal specialty is called *panado.* This Christmas tarte filled with apples may be set among the 13 desserts as a special treat.

The yule log tradition was once popular in many areas of France, including Provence. The custom may have developed from a medieval feudal tax called the "right of the log." Each Christmas Eve the peasants had to bring a mighty length of wood from the forest to the feudal lord's manor. Eventually, the people began ceremoniously bringing logs into their own homes at Christmas. Great ceremonies developed around how the log was to be blessed and how it was to be lighted.

In Provence, the lighting of the fire was called *cacho fio.* A yule log, often with the charred remains of the last Christmas Eve log, was laid on the hearth and set aflame. Everyone in the household gathered around to watch the ceremony, each with a glass of wine. The youngest member of the family dipped a twig into his or her glass and tossed the twig into the fire. The oldest, probably Grand-père, then hurled his glass into the flames as he recited a prayer. In one form or other, this prayer existed in most French provinces.

In Brittany, custom required that the eldest and youngest members of the family light the fire together. Then they offered the traditional prayer to Little Jesus. The Breton version of the blessing goes like this:

Christmas log, catch fire
Let us all rejoice.
Lord, give us Thy peace
And pour over us Thy blessing.

Lord, let us also
See the coming year.
And, if we are not one more,
May we not be one less.

The yule log was once an important Christmas tradition in Burgundy, too. In one town, a local castle supposedly had a log so large, a horse had to drag it through the great front door and all the way to the massive fireplace in the dining hall.

Before being put into the hearth, the yule log was sometimes used as a hiding place. On Christmas Eve, Burgundian fathers would tuck some goodies underneath the log: nuts, dried fruits, perhaps a coin. The children would go into another room to say their prayers to the Christ Child. They would come back when Papa called them and strike the log with a stick to make it give up what was "in its stomach." Then the children would search for the goodies.

Sometimes, Papa would tease the youngsters and put nothing at all under the log. He would tell the disappointed youngsters that they had not hit the log hard enough. Back to the other room they would go, to pray a little longer. Eventually, of course, Papa rewarded their efforts—or was it Little Jesus?

The yule log was a magical object, in Burgundy and other areas. One could gauge the harvest to come by striking the log's embers with tongs: the more the log crackled with sparks, the more sheafs of corn there would be. Once burned, the remaining cinders had medicinal powers. Put into the soil, they could prevent grain diseases. During storms, one had only to throw a handful of cinders into the hearth to keep lightning away from the house.

Besides the yule log, one of the more widespread traditions in Burgundy was the "singing quest," which took place on Christmas Eve, before the log was placed in the hearth. Youngsters ran through the streets of towns and villages carrying lighted candles and singing carols. They would stop at every shop—the butcher's, the baker's, the grocer's—to beg for treats. The children continued their quest until their candles were burned down to the nubs. This search was supposed to commemorate Joseph and Mary's journey from house to house, seeking lodging on the Holy Night.

Another Burgundian custom was especially picturesque. Children in some towns made small sacks from paper. Inside, they would tuck a coin. On Christmas Eve, the youngsters stood in their windows and tossed the sacks into the dark streets, first lighting one corner of the bag. Those in need could easily find the gifts, guided by the lights—like tiny shooting stars.

Grand-mère carries on the tradition of her Provençal forebearers by presenting the 13 desserts that will cap the réveillon.

The Burgundians cherished the Christmas holiday, so much so that the name of the Christmas season itself was used as a year-round cheer. People cried "Noël, Noël!" to greet passing nobility or other distinguished persons. The greeting was also commonly used for almost every special occasion—at marriages, births, even the signing of peace treaties.

In France, almost everyone attends one of the midnight Masses on Christmas Eve. The services range from grandly impressive ones in mighty cathedrals, where choirs sing to the deep tones of ancient organs, to simple observances in village churches.

In the extreme northeast of Alsace, on the German border, Mass is celebrated in an historic convent church high on the mountain of Sainte-Odile, above Strasbourg and the Rhine River. On Christmas Night, the beautiful old church's illumination can be seen for many miles, into the countryside of both Germany and France.

South of Paris, in the Loire Valley, visitors are invited to hear magnificent Gregorian chants sung at the 1,000-year-old Benedictine church at Saint-Benoît-sur-Loire, and at the Benedictine abbey in Solesmes, first built in 1010.

On the island of Corsica, in the Mediterranean Sea, the capital of Ajaccio offers a completely different type of Christmas music. There, churches ring with ancient Corsican carols, showing the influence of Italy, which once ruled the island.

At the church of Saint-Benoît du Cap-d'Antibes, in Provence, worshipers are invited to see a European crèche made with characters representing all the countries of Old Europe. And nearby, at La Colle-sur-Loup, the faithful may observe a Tahitian Noël.

To make sure absolutely no one is left out, the airport in Nice has provided Mass in the terminal for travelers unlucky enough to be away from home on the Holy Night.

Services are advertised all over the country: in the newspapers, on the airwaves, and on posters or fliers, which are popular French vehicles for announcing events. A few posters even include a poetic touch and a timely message to the reader. This one is for the Christmas Eve services at the church of Saint-Antoine Ginestière, in Nice:

Noël, for some, is pleasure, parties, the réveillon, skiing. Let us not permit these pleasures to make us thoughtless. The "alarm bells" ring out at Christmas to alert our hearts: Let us share the sufferings of those sick, alone, at war. But let us also share our joys with them. Then, the true joy of Christmas is in us.

The charming announcement continues:

We suggest that you come to express this joy by joining our chorale, which, after 11 o'clock tonight, will begin the Christmas Eve service. Then, by the light of candles, "Oh, Holy Night" will arise, demonstrating the intense emotions of our souls. After will come the moment of meditation: the midnight Mass, where each, in communion with all, will pray according to his own heart. Come find the joy that Jesus offers you and celebrate with us the coming to earth of the Son of God.

The poster's message concludes with one final, practical note:

Paix et joie! Parking spacieux et gratuit.
Peace and joy! Spacious, free parking lot.

Especially in the cities of France, many of the old ways of observing Christmas threaten to disappear. Much of the countryside, however, still clings to ancient rituals and pageantry. The carolers, the pastorales, the living crèches, the pilgrimages, the traditional réveillon foods—all combine to create a holiday that hearkens back to celebrations many hundreds of years in the past.

Everywhere, churches overflow with worshipers on Christmas Eve. Families gather later, sharing the Holy Night. The customs are beautiful, all blending together to create the joyous celebration called Noël.

A new generation in Arles gathers before the family hearth in anticipation of Père Noël.

THE SANTONS OF PROVENCE

The santons of Provence are the heart of French Noël. The simplicity of these manger figures, the rural charm of their humble dress, their incredible variety are unique.

All the characters of the old French countryside are found among the santons, or little saints. Placed in the crèche, they resemble real people, in the detail of their expressions and in their clothes. There is the heavy garlic woman, with her warts and wrinkles, and the mayor in his tidy dress. The fisherwoman appears, her basket full of catches from the sea, and so do the gypsies in their colorful clothes and jewelry. A shepherd stands among the santons, a lamb in his arms. The shepherdess stands beside him, perhaps chatting with the village gossip.

Many of the santons are placed so that they are on their way to see Little Jesus in the manger. A drummer boy leads them, and a boy with a fife. Each santon has a gift to offer the Christ Child in His manger: a chicken, a basket of fruit, some flowers. The town simpleton is always the exception: he can only throw up his hands in amazement that the Son

of God has come to earth. And the blind man, also present, has nothing to offer but a prayer.

The gifts from the santons are not so precious as those of the Three Kings, also represented at the crèche. But the presents of the folk are far more touching—simple gifts, given wholeheartedly by simple people.

No one is excluded: the baker, the pastry maker and the hunter, who turns aside his gun. Even unsavory characters—convicts, thieves, and pickpockets— may take their place in the crèche, making it a true representation of society.

The history of the santons began in the early 1800's, when a group of Italian peddlers came to

In a Provençal crèche, these costumed santons move toward the manger to make their humble offering to Little Jesus (above). In Aubagne, Monsieur Chave established this santon work- shop in 1932 (right).

A santon maker in Marseille unmolds a clay santon, the favorite of France (top). A worker paints the clay figures with great care in Toulon (middle). The Marseille santon fair finds Castelin-Peirano's stall offering dozens of both clay and costumed santons (bottom).

Marseille. The peddlers brought with them small, brightly painted figures made of clay, which they sold in the city's streets and markets.

Local artisans were so delighted with the little figures that they began to make santons, too, in French dress of the period. Artisans have been doing so ever since, and their work is considered some of the finest in the world.

The santons are a true regional art form. No matter how many versions of the crèche one may see in France today, the classic French manger scene is the one that includes the exquisite santons of Provence.

There are two types of santons: the *santons d'argile,* clay figures, and the *santons habillés,* clothed figures. The clothed are delightful, like dolls. But they take second place to the beloved clay santons.

Making santons is a family occupation in Provence, with everyone helping out in some way. Many santon makers are the product of several generations of artisans, from great-grandfather down. Creating the figures is a difficult, time-consuming art, taught by fathers and mothers to the youngsters, who assist after school and during vacations.

There are some first-generation santon makers, but the art is not easy to learn as an adult. Many of the "new" santon makers have married into families of santon artisans.

The clay figures are molded in two halves; when they are pressed together, the clay fuses into a whole. Then the artist creates exactly the appearance or expression he wants. Separate parts such as hats, baskets, and other accessories are attached to the body with a special adhesive.

As the figure dries and hardens, it gradually changes color. When completely dry, it is given a bath in a solution of gelatin to harden it further and to give it a special gloss. This covering provides a good surface for the application of coloring pigments. Without it, the colors would run.

Then the santons are lined up in rows, one type of character per row. All the millers will be together, for instance, or all the winemakers. Their faces are painted first, then the hair and the clothing and any accessories.

Until the end of the 1800's, clay santons were not fired in kilns, but merely dried in the sun. Even as late as 1945, many santon makers clung to the old open-air tradition. A few still do today. But the classic, old-style santons are so fragile that they tend to break, so most santon makers now usually fire them for longer life and durability.

Each year in Marseille a special santon fair is held. It is an old fair, dating back to 1803. There are not many santon makers, and only a few dozen come to

The candid simplicity of this grouping of clay santons is the essence of Noël to the French people.

set up their displays in Les Allées, the market spot where the fair takes place.

Over a hundred different types of clay and clothed santons may be exhibited at one stand—a full year's work. Each santon maker has a separate stand, with the family on hand to help with the sales. All are proud of their work, and, if asked about their background, may reply, *"Moi? Je suis né à la foire!"* or "Me? I was born at the fair!"

The setting of the French crèche is seldom that of ancient Bethlehem. The santons are instead placed in the French countryside, where they belong. With them, there will be animals, too: the ox and the donkey are especially important. It is their breath that warms the Christ Child.

There are other animals of the farmlands: dogs, cats, pigs, horses, sheep, and lambs. Sometimes, the santon makers import animals from exotic areas. There may be camels, elephants, or a leopard or two mingling with the other figures.

Many magnificent antique crèches with their lovely santons are seen today in churches and in homes. Museums particularly treasure them and carefully preserve the crèches, bringing them out each year for all to admire.

The church at Beausset in Provence has a crèche more than 100 years old. Its santons are reunited only at Christmastime. The rest of the year, the treasured figures are scattered among the different families of the village, who care for them with great affection.

Another marvelous manger scene is at the church of Saint-Antoine Ginestière, in Nice. The background is a miniature medieval castle, set on a mountaintop.

And, in Vaucluse, at La Crémade, there is a crèche to rival any of the others. The spectacular manger scene is rebuilt each year by devoted artisans. Every Christmas the crèche is given a different setting to represent one of the villages of Comtat Venaissin.

To be sure, there are crèches in France that differ from the traditional Provençal type. They appear made of wood, paper, and porcelain. Some have been composed of innovative materials such as sugar lumps and breadcrumbs. Knitted and crocheted figures take their place occasionally. There are even animated crèches, such as the one found in the tiny church atop a hill overlooking the old quarter of Cannes, on the Riviera. A series of weights and pulleys move its figures. As the images reenact the Nativity scene, a chorus of angels sings.

But, innovation aside, the French always go back to their favorite when thinking of the crèche as it should be: a place of simplicity, where everyone belongs. They think of the crèche of Provence. There, all the humble santons stand near the Christ Child, Who welcomes them all.

CHRISTMAS, THE FRENCH WAY

Shopping is done, and darkness has settled over the market places. It is Christmas Eve, and the spirit of Little Jesus is coming to France. The house becomes peaceful as the children, ringed by older members of the family, place the figure of the Christ Child into the crèche.

With luck, all the family members are there. The children put their shoes at the hearth with assurance from the grown-ups that Jesus will fill the shoes up by morning. Someone will explain how once, long ago, Jesus Himself and some of His angels came to the hearth. These days, however, Jesus sends Père Noël in His place. Why? Well . . . no one really knows.

A tree stands in the corner, its bulbs and tinsel reflecting the flickering candles on the mantle. Spaces have been left empty in the tree so Père Noël can leave goodies and toys there, too, for the children.

In the arms of an uncle, or maybe a big sister, a four-year-old nods sleepily while listening to a Christmas story. It may be the legend of John Red-Throat, who on Christmas helps little boys or girls in need. Maman begins to place flowers about the room, and someone reminds the children of another legend: the one that tells how on Christmas Night, Little Jesus once sent the Christmas rose to save a young man's soul.

Near a window, an older brother is examining a makeshift indoor wheat garden, now shorn. The children planted the wheat in a small container at the window on December 4, the feast day of Saint Barbara. The green shafts were tall by early Christmas Eve. Just a few hours before, the older children snipped the shoots and carried them to the crèche, careful not to bruise them. The children placed the shoots into the manger so that Little Jesus would find a soft bed when He arrived. The rest of the wheat shoots went in between the crèche figures; candles were placed on the soft green relief. Now the faces of the manger figures glow in the light of the small tapers lined up in front of the crèche.

There is more to come this Christmas Night. The children will sing some of the beloved Christmas songs that go far back into French history. There is the lullaby about the donkey and the ox, who watch over Jesus in the manger, warming Him with their breath as He falls to sleep. French children have sung this song for 700 years, each Christmas Night. Then there is the song about the angels who came to seek the shepherds in the countryside, telling them that the Christ Child is born. Someone might remember the song about Jeannette, too, who takes her torch so she can see her way to the manger to find Little Jesus.

Maman announces that the time has come for the little ones to go to bed. She has been wearing an apron most of the day because of all the activity in the kitchen. A white tablecloth already stands on the dining room table. In the middle is a floral centerpiece. Among the fresh blossoms candles wait to be lighted for the réveillon, which will take place after Mass.

Then Papa remembers that the children have left out one important step in the Christmas preparations—the snack for Père Noël and his donkey. Off to the kitchen the older children go to select something delicious to place at the hearth.

Finally, the youngsters are tucked in between the covers to dream of the good things to come Christmas morning. Downstairs, the rest of the family settle back to some good conversation, a few jokes, and a nibble of food before going to midnight Mass.

Noël has come to France once again. The spirit of Little Jesus will find the family wrapped in the warmth of togetherness yet another time.

The wings of heavenly companions rustle softly around Jesus as he fills the little shoes on Christmas night.

For almost 15 centuries, the French have celebrated Christmas in their unique way. The long history of the holiday has given it a character unlike that of any other holiday in France.

Though traditions vary somewhat throughout the country, there are some unwavering rules of thumb for those who wish to recreate the French celebration. Serving a lavish réveillon is one of them; preparing the home just right for the holiday is another. And, to surround the whole celebration, the refrains of beloved Christmas songs are a must.

Observing Christmas the French way is a matter of meeting these three requirements and one more—perhaps the most important. Christmas is a day especially for the children, but it is also a time for the family to share. There is a place in it for everyone, from the oldest to the very youngest.

A good example from the past of family togetherness on Christmas Night comes from the province of Auvergne, in the mountains of south-central France. Here, the *veillée,* or Christmas Eve vigil, found all the family members reunited.

The dinner table, set before the hearth, was covered with a white tablecloth on top of which stood a magnificent *brioche,* a kind of bread rich in eggs and butter. In the center of the brioche was a brass candlestick, rubbed to its highest polish. Nearby was a brand-new candle trimmed in tinsel: the Christmas candle.

As the time for réveillon approached, everyone gathered at the table in the darkened room. In Auvergne, even the very youngest took part in the feast. Then a lovely ceremony began, passed down from generation to generation for hundreds of years.

The oldest member of the family would put the candle into the candlestick, light the candle, and make the sign of the cross. Then the elder would put the candle out, passing it to the oldest son.

The ceremony was repeated as the candle passed from the oldest son to his wife, and on. In large families, the ceremony was not a quick affair. It unfolded gradually as the flame went from one beloved relative to the next and the embers of the yule log popped in the hearth.

At last, the candle went to the last-born grandchild. If the child was quite young, the mother would place the candle in the child's left hand, wrapping her own hand over so the youngster would have a steadier grip. Then she would help him or her to light the candle. Other members of the family would encourage the child and mother and also offer warnings about holding the candle straight, keeping its flame far away from clothing and eyes, and avoiding any dripping wax that threatened blisters.

Then, the flame still burning, the child made the sign of the cross, mother guiding the little hand in the right directions. That step completed, it was time for the candle to be placed into the candlestick. The mother helped the youngster lean over the table, both of them stretching toward the brioche. One firm shove and the candle was in place. Applause came from all gathered there, and a candlelit réveillon began.

French families love good food at Christmas and, for that matter, all year round. But, rather than having five or six courses, with large portions of each, the French prefer smaller helpings of a dozen or more delectable dishes. Such a meal will not be gobbled down in the space of 30 minutes or so. Instead, the banquet will go on much longer, even for hours.

Maman is very busy the entire time. She prepares only some of the food beforehand and so can never sit down for the duration of the meal. Besides, few tables have space enough for a dozen courses of food, and hot plates can do only so much to keep the food at its peak as the meal continues. For Maman, réveillon is strictly a cook-as-you-go situation.

Another reason for Maman's whirlwind activity during réveillon is the problem of dishes and eating utensils. Sitting down at the table, each reveler will find a neat stack of dishes and an assortment of forks and spoons. These are whisked away as the courses are served. Unless a family has a warehouse of china and silverware, there will be mid-réveillon dishwashings to insure a steady flow of place settings as the guests dine through the night.

And then there is the question of glasses. In many families, a different wine is served with each new course. Wine stems therefore must also be changed, so as not to mix the delicate flavors of the wines. One effective strategy for eliminating this problem is to serve only champagne. Cost and family preference permitting, Maman and Papa will take this detour around growing stacks of used drinking vessels.

Réveillon frequently opens with a French favorite—shellfish. The first course may therefore find Maman, perhaps with Papa's help, opening oysters in the kitchen. The succulent mollusks on their bed of ice are brought into the dining room with great fanfare, accompanied by oil and vinegar, and also lemon wedges. Other condiments could be served, but the lemon and vinaigrette enhance rather than dwarf the oysters' subtle flavor.

Next come canapés in profusion: green stuffed olives covered with cream cheese and rolled in chopped walnuts; mushroom caps stuffed with remoulade dressing; tiny tomatoes filled with garlicky cream cheese and topped with ripe, black olives. The canapés are one course Maman may have prepared in advance. Still, the table must be cleared of platters and dishes from the first course to make room for the new offering. This is especially true because along with the canapés come the hors d'oeuvres: hard cooked eggs, which also lend themselves to early preparation.

Eggs mimosa and mushroom eggs are two favorites that might appear on the réveillon table. Eggs mimosa are French-style deviled eggs, spiced with Dijon mustard and chives, then mellowed with a trace of garlic. Mushroom eggs contain the same ingredients as eggs mimosa, but they stand on their ends, not on their sides, and have a red cap of tomato shell. The egg course makes for a festive presentation, with the white and red of the basic ingredients, plus fresh green garnishes.

No réveillon is complete without pâtés. There are several varieties of this exquisite meat spread. One, pâté de foie gras, is a hands-down favorite. It is made from goose liver and delicate herbs. If Maman is ambitious, she has carved the chilled pâté into the shape of a yule log, adding yet another creative touch to the table. Also, a holiday beauty is a pâté of duck, served in a long casserole dish and topped with a flaky pie crust.

An easy-to-cook pâté of universal popularity is rilletes, made of pork, onions, garlic, and herbs. This pâté is served in crockery jars. The guests pass the jars around, spooning the spread onto their bread dish. Then, they break a small piece from their chunk of crusty baguette—a long, thin French bread. Morsel of baguette in hand, they pop a teaspoon of rillettes on with their knife, and into the mouth goes the aromatic combination.

MENU

Oysters on the half shell

Assorted canapés

Eggs mimosa

Mushroom eggs

Assorted pâtés

Rillettes

Twice-stuffed turkey

Sweet peas à la française
in nests of duchess potatoes

Remoulade salad

Assorted cheeses

Winter fruits

Bûche de Noël

Coffee

Cointreau   Cognac

While this is going on, Maman is in the kitchen—again. A half hour earlier, somewhere between the eggs and the pâté, Papa removed the réveillon bird from the oven. This year it is a plump, twice-stuffed turkey, baked with chestnut stuffing and herb stuffing until its skin is a crinkly brown. Maman puts more chestnuts and other garnishes all around the bird—treats to pique the guests' appetites as they dig into the stuffing and select among juicy slices of white and dark meat.

With the bird comes a wine sauce to bring out the flavor of the chestnuts and meat. And, as a perfect complement, there are duchess potatoes topped with sweet peas.

Early in the day, while stuffing the turkey, Maman also prepared the mixture for the duchess potatoes. It turned out to be quite like mashed potatoes, only there were eggs and a touch of onion added for creaminess and flavor. The mixture complete, she placed it into a forcing bag and then made little nests of potatoes in a large crockery dish. Now, the nests have been baked to a golden brown. In them, Maman places the butter-laden peas, flavored with sweet, tiny onions and the taunting juices from simmered Bibb lettuce. The casserole is a spring basket as Maman places it next to the bird.

Considerable time passes between the turkey and the next course as the guests slowly clean their plates and wait for all to settle so they can perhaps try a few more nibbles. The conversation ebbs and then becomes animated as an interesting new topic is introduced. With determination, Maman rises from the table again, this time to tackle the remoulade salad.

Remoulade is a dressing made with grated celery root, a vegetable whose quality remains unsung in many parts of the world, even where it is available in quantity. The texture is crisp, the flavor fruity and light. Mixed with spicy mayonnaise—the same Maman made to use in the eggs mimosa, mushroom eggs, and canapés—celery root is an inexpensive base for a refreshing remoulade.

Maman lines a salad bowl with red leaf lettuce, then centers Boston lettuce in the bowl. The remoulade goes on the Boston lettuce, and, for eye appeal, a few retrieved tendrils of celery root are posed on the red leaf lettuce. The réveillon salad is served.

Almost unbelievably, the time comes for more: assorted cheeses, winter fruits, and nuts—all served together.

French cheeses are as varied as French Christmas customs. The more varieties offered at the réveillon table, the better. Then the guests can pick and choose, comparing the merits of the individual cheeses while savoring them along with morsels of bread and unsalted butter. It is important that fine cheeses be served at room temperature, and only unsalted butter should appear with them. Chilling and salt attack the flavor of the cheeses, deadening the palate to their creamy deliciousness.

Actually, for best results, all courses should be lightly salted; and, if not specifically meant to be served warm, they should be served at room temperature. This caution applies to many canapés and hors d'oeuvres, some pâtés, salads, cheeses, and fruits.

This year's cheese assortment begins with *Roquefort*, standing like a crumbling marble wedge amid the others. Then there is *Brie*, which has been made in France since the twelfth century. Brie tastes like a very thick, sweet cream, and is a good companion to *Saint Paulin*, which is firm, with a touch of bitterness as its flavor lingers on the tongue. *Boursin*, wrapped in crushed pepper or herbs, has a subtle sweetness, like fine cream cheese; and *Gourmandise* is present in three different flavors—walnut, cherry, and orange.

Camembert is full of surprises. If fresh, this disk, with its moldy crust, contains a creamy cheese with a pungent flavor. If allowed to ripen, the cheese begins to break down in the center until it literally runs from a cut wedge. The runny part is scooped onto bread, perhaps with some of the crust, said to be healthful due to its high calcium content. Fresh or ripe, few guests will ever pass up the Camembert.

With luck, there will be yet another, rarer cheese on the platter: *Doux de montagne*. This cheese is riddled with little holes and has the flavor of fine buttermilk.

Though not many réveillon hostesses will be able to turn out this lavish a spread of cheeses, all can find an assortment of winter fruits to serve—the riper the better. There are grapes, red and white, juicy pears, and tart or sweet apples. These fruits and other family favorites are served on the stem and whole, with a side dish of walnut halves. Guests cut up their own selections, popping down the orbs and slices along with the crunchy nuts.

A fair guess is that Maman is tired by now, but this is not the time to lose heart. The moment has come for the presentation of a magnificent bûche de Noël—the Christmas yule log.

This confection represents the traditional yule log once burned in French hearths on Christmas Eve. With the disappearance of fireplaces and the coming of other heating systems, the French were loath to give up the beloved tradition of the log. So, we find it today served in the form of a chocolaty dessert.

A thin sponge cake is filled with chocolate butter cream and then rolled into a log and topped with more chocolate frosting. Running a fork over the frosting creates the texture of bark. Stumps of cake sit on the log, making it even more realistic. On the top, Maman has sprinkled powdered sugar to look like a layer of snow.

For hundreds of years, French families have gathered on Christmas Eve around the yule log. In this engraving from Alsace, a father blesses the log before igniting it.

There is holly—real or artificial—there, too, and little plastic elves or Père Noëls. To make the log look as if it really came from the forest, small mushrooms have been easily made from cream cheese. Stems are formed from the cooled cheese, then caps. Once the pieces are assembled and their tops rubbed in chocolate powder, the mushrooms are posed in several places on the log.

Sliced thinly, the pieces of swirled cake are served around as the guests settle down to this last course. Maman brings in the coffee, too, and Papa breaks out the Cointreau—for the women—and the Cognac, for the men. Toasts ring out, and the réveillon finally draws to a drowsy close.

Some homemakers are confronted with a dilemma each Christmas. Although turkey is a treasured main course for the several winter holidays, many families would prefer not having it twice.

For cooks who want to avoid this problem, here is another perfect recipe for the holiday bird: goose, stuffed with prunes and pâté. Do not be suspicious of this uncanny stuffing: it is an all-time favorite among the French at Christmastime, rich and flavorful with a red cabbage casserole, also featured here.

Roast goose
Prune and pâté stuffing

1 cup dry vermouth
2 cups beef bouillon
40 to 50 pitted prunes
12 to 14 pound goose
liver from goose, minced
2 tbs. minced onion
2 tbs. butter
1/3 cup port wine
8 oz. goose liver pâté
1 pinch allspice
1 pinch thyme
salt and pepper, to taste
1/2 cup bread crumbs
2 tart apples, cored and chopped

For sauce:
1/3 cup port wine

In saucepan, bring vermouth and beef bouillon to a boil. Place prunes into boiling liquid, cover saucepan, and reduce heat immediately. Simmer very slowly 10 minutes, until just tender. Drain and cool prunes. Reserve liquid. Wash goose thoroughly inside and out. Dry well. Remove excess fat from cavity. Saute liver from goose with shallots in 1 tablespoon butter for 2 minutes. Scrape into large mixing bowl. Add port to same skillet. Boil down to 2 tablespoons, scraping to deglaze. Add reduced port to mixing bowl. Add pâté, allspice, thyme, salt, and pepper. Mix thoroughly. Add bread crumbs and mix again. Saute apples in remaining tablespoon butter for 5 minutes. Add prunes and sauted apples to stuffing mixture at same time, gently stirring so prunes remain whole. Preheat oven to 325°. Salt goose cavity. Stuff loosely with prune mixture. Sew up and truss goose. Roast, uncovered, about 16 minutes per pound. Do not prick goose. Basting not required. Remove fat from pan periodically. Serves 8 to 10. For *sauce*, remove bird to platter. Remove excess fat from roasting pan. Deglaze pan, using reserved prune juice and port wine. Boil mixture down rapidly until flavor is full bodied, scraping roasting pan to get up drippings. Strain. If desired, thicken with cornstarch. Place in sauce boat. Serve with goose.

Baked red cabbage

4 strips bacon, chopped
1 cup onions, sliced
1/2 cup carrots, peeled and sliced
  crosswise
2 tbs. butter
2 lbs. red cabbage, cut into 1/2" slices
2 cups cored, diced apples (McIntosh
  recommended)
2 cloves garlic, minced
1 whole bay leaf
1 large pinch each, ground cloves,
  nutmeg, pepper
1/2 to 3/4 tsp. salt
2 cups dry red wine
2 cups beef bouillon
24 chestnuts, peeled (optional)

Preheat oven to 325°. Place bacon, onions, carrots, and butter into 10-quart pot. Cover and cook 10 minutes on stove over low flame. From cabbage, remove remnants of core and separate slices into strips. Place cabbage into pot and stir well. Cook covered 10 minutes more at same heat. Add other ingredients, stir, and cover. Bring mixture to simmer over low flame. Place mixture into 8-quart casserole, cover very tightly with both aluminum foil and a lid, and place in center of oven. Cook 5 hours. Correct salt and pepper to taste during cooking. Juices should evaporate completely. If not, uncover for last half-hour. Can be prepared ahead and reheated. Flavor improves with reheating. Serves 14. For variety, after cooking 3 1/2 hours, add chestnuts and return to oven for last 1 1/2 hours. (To peel chestnuts, pierce shells with nail or other sharply pointed object. Plunge chestnuts into boiling water until shells begin to split. Plunge into cold water. Remove shells when cooled.)

Decorating the home for Noël is a family activity in France, another example of the underlying tradition of togetherness at this time. How many frills are added for the holiday is a matter of family preference, of course; but many of the decorations are homespun, practical, and easy enough for the children to help create.

A manger scene is always present, but not usually under the tree. Instead, mother, with the children's help, places it in a prominent area, all by itself. A tabletop is a good choice; another is the hearth. Pine boughs and other natural touches may be added for authenticity. Candles are also present, to be lighted Christmas Night.

Custom has it that a basket of fruits should stand at the hearth. Flowers may be nearby, and also candy to tempt both grown-ups and youngsters.

Candles stand at the hearth, a symbol of hope. Holly could also be there, or pine boughs—tied with decorative bows. Mistletoe should hang somewhere in the room, also beribboned.

Though garlands and bulbs for the tree are usually bought in stores, other decorations are handmade. The children are especially encouraged to help with these, unless the decorations are meant as a surprise for the youngsters on Christmas morning. The children's participation provides them an opportunity to learn crafts like crocheting, sewing, knitting, tatting, paper art—the full spectrum.

Handmade ornaments include paper, crocheted, or foil stars. An easy and common craft is pine cone art. The cones are gathered from neighboring areas, if possible, painted, rubbed in glitter, and hung as ornaments. Another festive touch comes from little bows made of colorful ribbon. The bows are tied all over the branches.

Fruit has been associated with the tree from the beginning of its history in France. Apples, pears, and other types were once placed in the branches as presents for the children to find. Real fruit is difficult to pose in a tree, but artificial fruit may be created from a variety of materials.

Besides fruit, other goodies and small toys traditionally take their place in the tree. With ribbons, lollipops may be tied onto small branches. Also, small bags of nuts, chocolate coins, or chocolate candies can easily be made of plastic netting saved from grocery store produce bags. A piece of ribbon or string woven through the edges of a 7" circle of plastic netting makes for a good nut or candy pouch.

As a special surprise for the children, Père Noël dolls may be made of cloth or felt. These are given away to family children and also to visiting youngsters on Christmas Day.

French Christmas decorations are a creative challenge, very much a question of using available materials to their greatest advantage. The tricolored star, Père Noël ornament/pin, and kitchen clay fruit ornaments featured in the following pages are in the tradition of French decorations. The materials are easy to find and the instructions simple enough to permit even younger children to join in the holiday preparations.

Carols are another required feature when recreating an authentic French Christmas. Families sing the noëls, as the carols are called, in the home and also in churches on Christmas Eve.

Some of the noëls of French origin have a widespread popularity in other countries. One of these is "Angels we have heard on high"; another is the stirring "Oh, Holy Night."

Less well-known but of increasing popularity are "Bring a torch, Jeannette, Isabelle" and "Pat-a-pan." English versions of both these noëls are available in many record shops.

One carol that is inseparable from the Christmas celebration is of foreign origin: "Silent night," a German favorite. "Oh, Tannenbaum" is also widely sung.

The noëls featured in this section are probably the three most beloved to the French people. The first, "Sleep, Little Jesus," is from the thirteenth century, the era of Saint Francis of Assisi. The noël is a lullaby. Children sing it to Little Jesus in the manger each Christmas Night, assuring him of their devotion.

"Christ is born, play the music, sing!" comes from the reign of Louis XV in the eighteenth century. The tune was borrowed from an arrangement for hunting horns. The noël shows the traditional association between the royal winter hunts and the Christmas celebrations in France. The style is lively and joyous in this musical announcement that the Divine Child is born.

At last comes the beautiful "Oh, Holy Night." This carol from the nineteenth century is said to galvanize all the worshipers of France every Christmas Eve at midnight. The carol marks the official beginning of midnight Mass. For decades, it has been a moving statement of faith from the French people.

HOMESPUN TREASURES

Tricolored star

Assemble:
pencil, wax paper, carbon paper
cardboard, scissors, hole punch
2 sheets each, red, green,
white construction paper
4" x 4" piece clear vinyl or acetate
(mylar)
stapler, 9" fine metallic cord
2 metal rings, ½" diameter, pliers

1. Copy patterns on wax paper, doubling all dimensions. Using carbon paper, transfer doubled patterns to cardboard. Cut out patterns. Outline and cut 8 large pattern pieces of each color of construction paper (8 red, 8 green, 8 white). Punch holes where indicated on pattern. Cut 2 small pattern pieces of vinyl. Punch holes where indicated and put aside.

2. Place two large white pattern pieces aside. Divide other large pattern pieces in pairs of same color (4 red pairs, 4 green pairs, 3 white pairs). About ⅓ of the way up from the bottom of each pair, staple center together. Staple each pair together in identical spot.

3. In color sequence, staple sides of individual pattern pieces together, stapling the bottom piece of one color pair to the top piece of the next color pair. Color sequence is red/green/white/red. Repeat, making sure corner holes line up evenly.

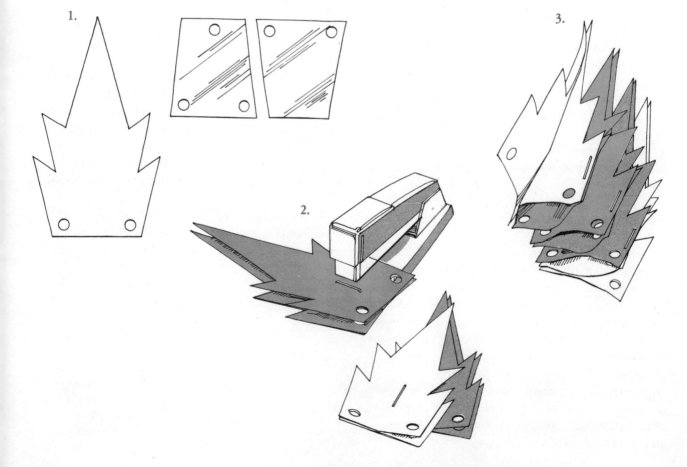

4.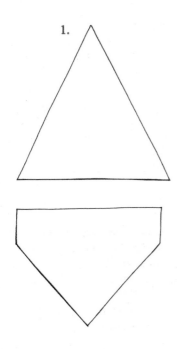

5.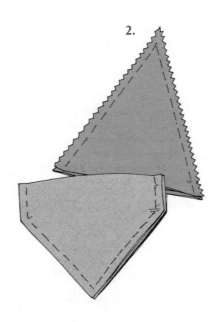

4. Assemble two extra white pattern pieces, two pieces of vinyl, and cord. Punch a hole near the top center of one piece of vinyl. Staple piece to one extra white pattern piece near top and bottom, making sure bottom holes line up. Repeat with other extra white pattern piece and vinyl, omitting hole punch step. Instead, with vinyl facing out, staple middle of cord to pieces. Tie loose end of cord into a knot. Vinyl facing out, staple two white pieces to other pieces at sides, one at each end. Open metal rings with pliers. Put through all holes in pattern pieces, one ring each side. Close rings tightly with pliers.

5. Pull knotted end of cord through hole in vinyl at opposite end. Ornament will unfold into a decorative star.

Père Noël ornament/pin

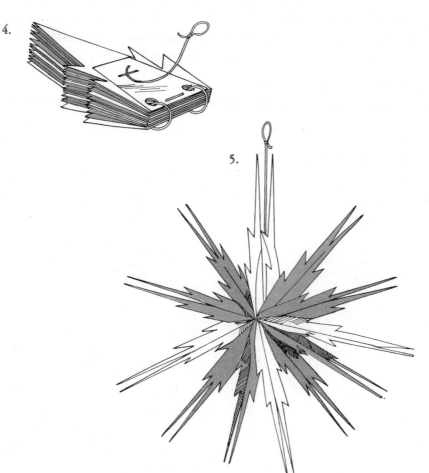

1.

2.

Assemble:

pencil, wax paper, scissors
5" x 8" rectangle each, red and skin-colored felt
straight pins, needle
red, skin-colored, and white thread
3 yds. white rug or craft yarn
scraps of black felt
white glue, cotton balls, large safety pins

1. Copy pattern for hat on wax paper. (If desired, size of Père Noël may be enlarged by increasing dimensions here and those for face, below.) Cut out pattern. Fold red felt in half. Pin pattern on doubled red felt and cut out 2 red felt pieces. Remove paper pattern. Repin 2 red felt pieces together.
2. Using red thread, sew red pieces together with a running stitch about ¼" from edge, leaving bottom open. For face pieces, repeat step 1 with

skin-colored felt, sewing sides together and leaving top open. Sew bottom of hat to top of face in front only.

3. For beard, take white rug yarn and make loops about 1" long. Stitch with white thread along edge of face. For features, cut out black felt eyes and red felt mouth. Use yarn for eyebrows. Attach features with white glue. For moustache, make a small bow of white yarn and sew on center of face.

4. At open back, stuff hat and face loosely with cotton balls. Sew up back.

5. Glue cotton balls along front seam where hat joins face. Glue one cotton ball at top of hat for pompon. Sew base of large safety pin to back of hat. Nestle Père Noël in tree as ornament to be given to children as lapel decoration.

3.

4.

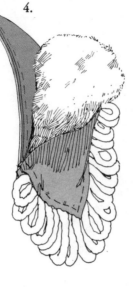

5.

Kitchen clay fruit ornaments

1.

Assemble:
1 cup salt, 2 cups flour
$1/2$ tsp. baking powder, 1 cup water
mixing bowl, mixing spoon

Mix salt, flour, and baking powder in bowl. Gradually stir in water. Knead mixture 5 to 10 minutes, until dough feels like clay. Flour hands frequently and liberally to keep clay from sticking. Yields 3 cups.

Assemble:
pencil, wax paper, scissors, flour
kitchen clay, small knife, toothpick
tempera paints, brush
clear nail polish, decorative cord

1. Trace fruit patterns on wax paper. Cut out patterns.

2.

3.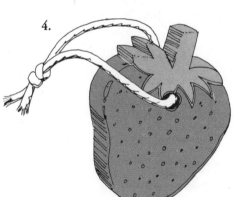

4.

2. Sprinkle flour liberally on work surface and hands. Take a small lump of clay and roll it into a ball between the hands. Flatten clay ball evenly with palm to $3/8$" thickness.

3. Place fruit pattern on flattened clay. Using knife, cut around edge. Remove pattern. With toothpick, draw interior details on fruit and make a hole near the top of fruit. Hole must be large enough to avoid closing up during drying. Repeat for other fruit patterns. If desired, create some original fruit or other ornament patterns for use with remaining clay.

4. Allow ornaments to air-dry for at least 48 hours. Paint ornaments. Allow ornaments to dry thoroughly again. Seal with coat of clear nail polish. Cut one 8" piece of cord for each ornament. Thread cord through hole. Knot ends together. Use cord to hang ornaments on tree.

Sing Noel!

Sleep, Little Jesus
Entre le boeuf et l'âne gris

Andante

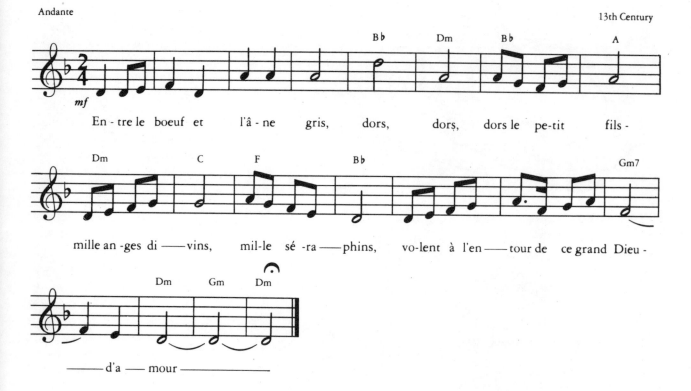

mf

En - tre le boeuf et l'â - ne gris, dors, dors, dors le pe-tit fils -

mille an -ges di — vins, mil-le sé -ra — phins, vo-lent à l'en — tour de ce grand Dieu -

— d'a — mour —

Ox and gray donkey bring Thee laud,
Sleep, sleep, little Lamb of God.
Angels all in rhyme, thousands at a time,
Sing to Thee, oh God of Love,
Emmanuel Divine.

Near rose and lily white as pearl,
Sleep, sleep, Savior of our world.
Angels in the sky, sing Thy lullaby,
Slumber in Thy manger,
Son of God on high.

Shepherds have come the Babe to find,
Sleep, sleep, hope of humankind.
Angels sing on high, shepherds pray nearby.
All is safe, so little Jesus
Close Thy eyes.

Christ Is Born, Play the Music, Sing!

Il est né, le divin Enfant

Refrain:
Christ is born, play the music, sing!
Bring out the pipes, beat the drum, together.
Christ is born, play the music, sing!
Raise your voices to praise our King.

Long ago in the Promised Land,
Prophets told of a Savior reigning.
Long ago in the Promised Land,
Christ the Lord came from heaven's hand.
(Refrain)

Humbly placed on a bed of straw,
Christ was born in a lonely stable.
Humbly placed on a bed of straw,
Christ the King came to save us all.
(Refrain)

Shout His glory and raise His song,
Pauper and prince hail the Son, your Savior.
Shout His glory and raise His song,
Join the praise of the mighty throng.
(Refrain)

Oh, Holy Night

Minuit, Chrétiens!

Larghetto

Adolphe Adam

Mi-nuit, chré -tiens, c'est l'heure so-len - nel - le où l'homme Dieu descen-dit jusqu'à nous pour ef-fa-

-cer — la tache o - ri - gi —nel — le et de son Père ar-rê —ter le cour — roux ————— le

monde en-tier tres—sail-le d'es-pé—ran—ce en cette nuit qui lui don - ne un sau—veur-

REFRAIN

Peuple à ge - noux ———— at-tends ———— ta dé-li—vran—ce No—ël ———— No-

-ël ———— Voi - ci ———— le rédemp - teur ———— No — ël ———— No — ël ———— Voi -

-ci ———— le rédemp — teur.

Oh, holy night, the stars are brightly shining,
It is the night of the dear Savior's birth.
Long lay the world in sin and error pining,
Till He appeared and the soul felt its worth.
A thrill of hope, the weary world rejoices,
For yonder breaks a new and glorious morn.
    Fall on your knees!
    Oh, hear the angel voices!
    Oh, night divine;
    Oh, night when Christ was born.
    Oh, night divine!
    Oh, night. Oh, night divine!

Led by the light of faith serenely beaming,
With glowing hearts by His cradle we stand;
So led by light of a star sweetly gleaming,
Here came the Wise Men from Orient land.
The King of Kings lay thus in lowly manger,
In all our trials born to be our friend.
    He knows our need,
    To our weakness is no stranger.
    Behold your King!
    Before Him lowly bend!
    Behold your King!
    Before Him lowly bend!

Truly He taught us to love one another;
His law is love, and His gospel is peace.
Chains shall He break, for the slave is our brother,
And in His name all oppressions shall cease.
Sweet hymns of joy in grateful chorus raise we,
Let all within us praise His holy name.
    Christ is the Lord,
    Oh, praise His name forever!
    His power and glory
    Evermore proclaim!
    His power and glory
    Evermore proclaim!

Acknowledgments

Cover: Photo by Dean Jacobson

2: B. C. Press, Rapho/Photo Researchers
6: Musée Jacquemart-André (J. E. Bulloz)
8: Belzeaux, Rapho/Photo Researchers
9: © John Topham Picture Library
10: Dennis Mansell
11: Dennis Mansell
12: © Joseph F. Viesti (World Book photo); © Joseph F. Viesti (World Book photo)
13: © Gaston Malherbe from Louis Mercier
14: © Joseph F. Viesti (World Book photo)
15: © Gaston Malherbe from Louis Mercier
17: © J. J. Damiani; © Gaston Malherbe from Louis Mercier
18: Dennis Mansell
19: Dennis Mansell; Dennis Mansell
20: Dennis Mansell; © Gaston Malherbe from Louis Mercier
21: © Gaston Malherbe from Louis Mercier
22: Hervé Donnezan, Rapho/Photo Researchers
23: S. Weiss, Rapho/Photo Researchers
24: © Joseph F. Viesti and J. J. Damiani (World Book photo); © Gaston Malherbe from Louis Mercier
25: Bajande, Rapho/Photo Researchers
26: © Joseph F. Viesti (World Book photo)
27: Feher, Rapho/Photo Researchers; © Joseph F. Viesti (World Book photo)
28: The Granger Collection, New York
29: Musée des Beaux-Arts, Reims (Giraudon)
30: Mary Evans Picture Library
32: James M. Curran
33: Historical Pictures Service, Inc.
34: Historical Pictures Service, Inc.
35: Musée Condé, Chantilly (Giraudon)
36: © Edouard Berne, fotogram from John Topham Picture Library
37: © Edouard Berne, Fotogram from John Topham Picture Library
38: © Joseph F. Viesti (World Book photo)
39: © Gaston Malherbe from Louis Mercier; © Gaston Malherbe from Louis Mercier

40: © J. J. Damiani
41: © J. J. Damiani; M. Kerdiles, Rapho/Photo Researchers
42: © F. Loucel, John Topham Picture Library
43: Agence Française d'Illustration Photographique
44: © Joseph F. Viesti (World Book photo)
46: © Joseph F. Viesti (World Book photo)
47: Serraillier, Rapho/Photo Researchers; Rapho/Photo Researchers
48: Rapho/Photo Researchers
49: © 1979 George Elich; © Joseph F. Viesti (World Book photo)
50: © Gaston Malherbe from Louis Mercier; H. Briliat, Rapho/Photo Researchers
52: © Gaston Malherbe from Louis Mercier
53: Marc Tulane, Rapho/Photo Researchers
54: © Jean Ribière
56: © J. J. Damiani
57: © Joseph F. Viesti (World Book photo)
58: Halin, Rapho/Photo Researchers
59: © Gaston Malherbe from Louis Mercier
60: Agence Française d'Illustration Photographique; © Gaston Malherbe from Louis Mercier; © Gaston Malherbe from Louis Mercier
61: World Book photo by Free Chin
62-63: Ronis, Rapho/Photo Researchers
64: Historical Pictures Service, Inc.
69: Photo Rigal, Editions Arthaud, Paris
72-75: James M. Curran
76-78: William Chin
Note: Credits should be read from left to right, top to bottom, on their respective pages.

The stories "The Christmas Rose" (pp. 11-12) and "The Réveillon of Piboule" (pp. 52-54) are adapted from Maguelonne Toussaint-Samat, *Légendes et récits du temps de Noël* (Paris: Fernand Nathan, Editeur 1977).